Transcribed SCORES™

T H E B E

Blood, Sweat & Tears

HAL•LEONARD® CORPORATION

7777 W. Bluemound Rd. P.O. Box 13819 Milwaukee, WI 53213

AND WHEN I DIE

Words and Music by
LAURA NYRO

17 Faster ♩ = 126
Tacet 1st x
Synth.
Vocal
If it's peace you find in dy - in'; well, then let the time be near. If it's peace you find in
Harm.
Piano
A6 D6 A6 D6 A6 D6 Bm7/E D6 A6 G
Bass
Drums
(4)
(8)
Synth.
Vocal
dy - in' and if dy - in' time is near, just bun - dle up my cof - fin' 'cause it's cold way down
Harm.
Piano
D G D Esus Bm7 C♯m7 D D/E A D
Bass
Drums

Synth.
Vocal
there, I hear_ that it's cold way down there. Yeah, ___ cra - zy cold way down there. ___
Harm.
Piano
A D A D A Dmaj7 C♯m7 Bm7 D/E A D
Bass
(4)
Drums
To Coda
31
Play
And when I die, ___ and when I'm gone, ___ There'll be one child born in this
A D A Bm7 C♯m7 F♯m7 A7 Dmaj7 C♯m7 Bm7 D/E
(8)
(4)

as played by Dick Halligan
43
8va
Solo
To Piano Sound
"Rinky Tink" Piano Sound
Synth.
Vocal
world to car - ry on, to car - ry on.
Harm.
A D D A A D D A
Piano
Bass
A D D A A D D A A
Drums
D A D A D A
(4)

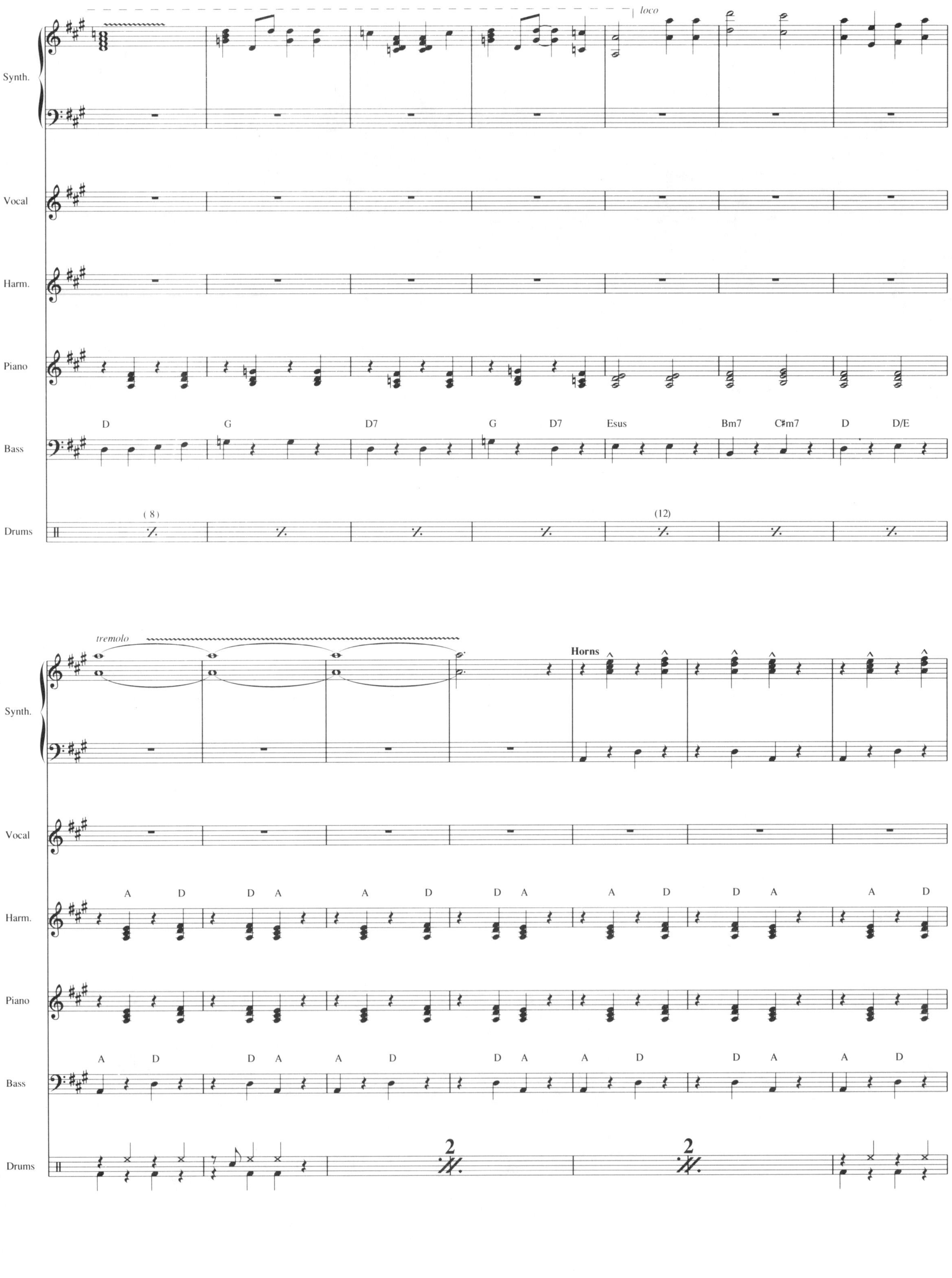
loco
Synth.
Vocal
Harm.
Piano
D G D7 G D7 Esus Bm7 C♯m7 D D/E
Bass
(8)
(12)
Drums
tremolo
Horns
A D D A A D D A A D D A A D
2
2

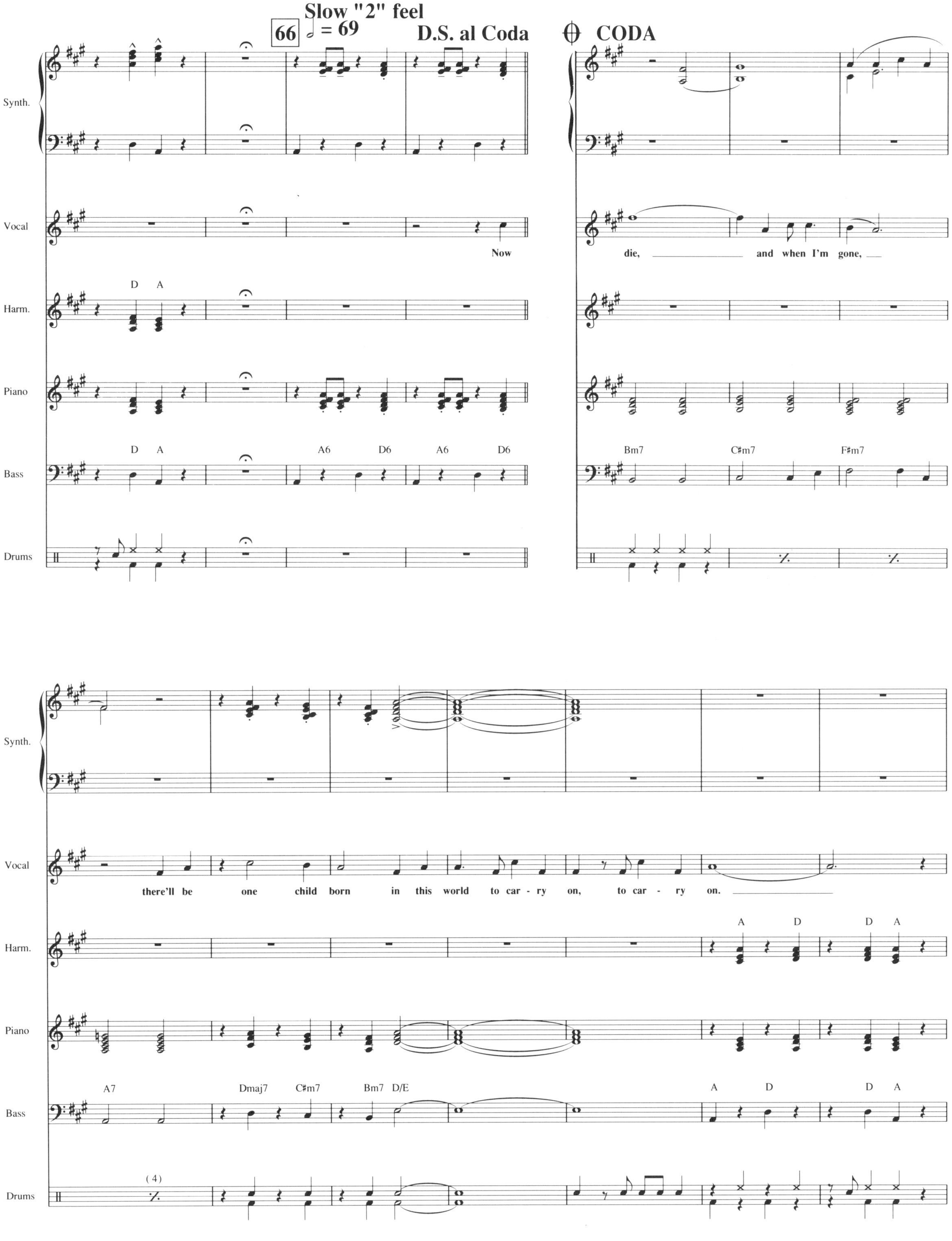
Slow "2" feel
66
𝅗𝅥 = 69
D.S. al Coda
CODA
Synth.
Vocal
Harm.
Piano
Bass
Drums
D A
A6 D6 A6 D6
Now
die, and when I'm gone,
Bm7 C♯m7 F♯m7
there'll be one child born in this world to car - ry on, to car - ry on.
A7 Dmaj7 C♯m7 Bm7 D/E
A D D A
(4)

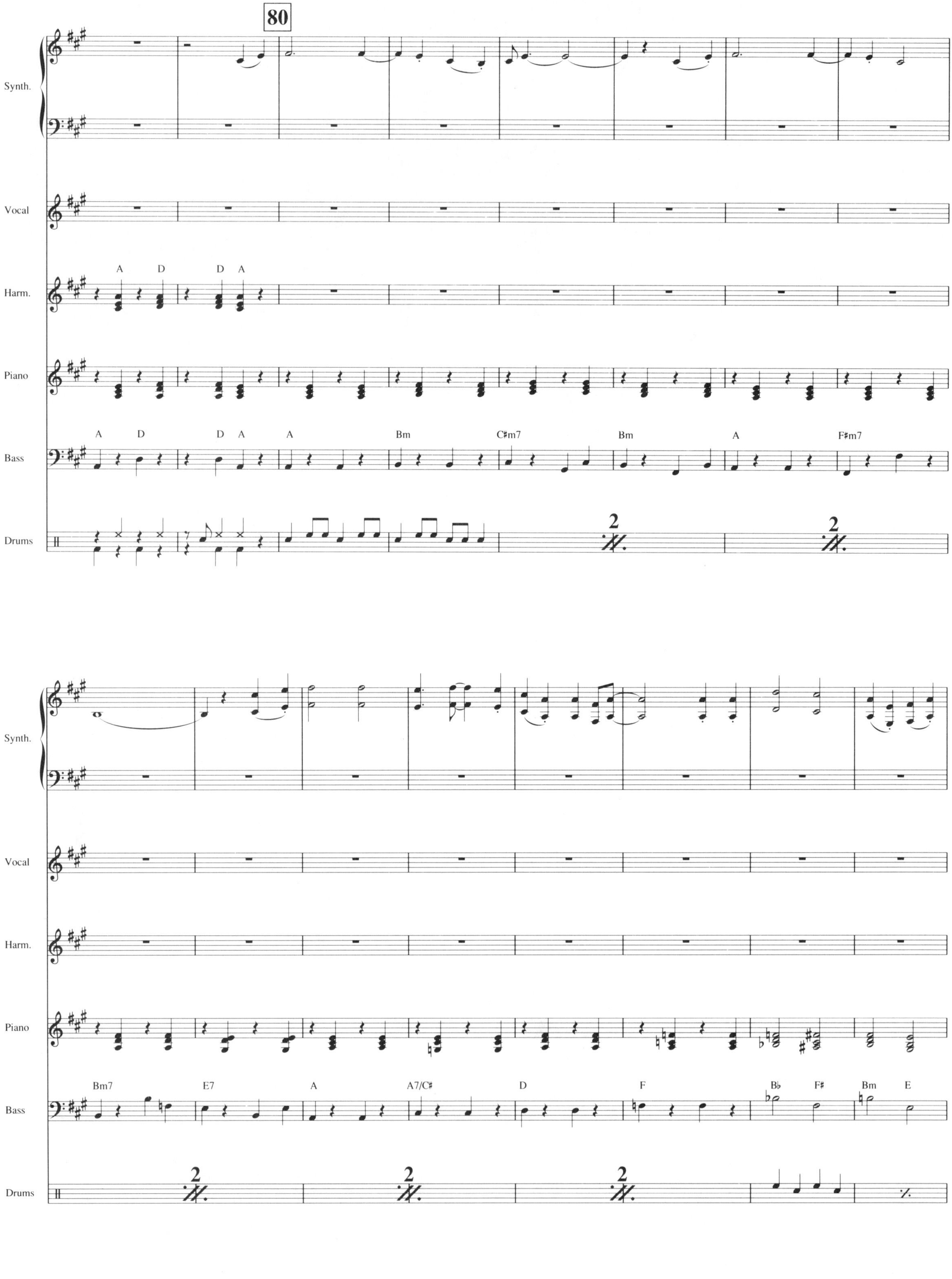
80
Synth.
Vocal
Harm.
A D D A
Piano
Bass
A D D A A Bm C#m7 Bm A F#m7
Drums
2
2
Synth.
Vocal
Harm.
Piano
Bass
Bm7 E7 A A7/C# D F B♭ F# Bm E
Drums
2
2
2

Synth.
Vocal
Harm.
A D D A A D D A A D D A A D D A
Piano
Bass
A D D A A D D A A D D A A D D A
Drums
2
2
2
103
𝅗𝅥 = 69
Slow "2" feel
Synth.
Vocal
Give me my free - dom for as long as I be; all I ask of liv - in' is to
Harm.
Piano
p
Bass
A6 D6 A6 D6 A6 D6 A6 D6 A6 D6 A6 D6
p
Drums

111 Faster 𝅗𝅥 = 126
Synth.
Vocal
have no chains _ on me. All I ask of liv - in' is ___ to have no chains on
Harm.
Piano
Bm7/E D6 A6 G D G D
Bass
Drums
Synth.
Vocal
me, ______ And all I ask of dy - in' is to go nat - 'ral - ly, ___ I on - ly wan - na go nat - 'ral - ly. _
Harm.
Piano
Esus Bm7 C♯m7 D D/E A D A D A D
Bass
Drums

121
Half Tempo Rock
Synth.
Vocal
Harm.
Piano
Bass
Drums
Here I go!
here come the dev - il
right be - hind
A
A7
(4)

129
Double Time
Synth.
Vocal
Harm.
Piano
Bass
Drums
A
Don't wan-na go by the dev-il; don't _ wan-na go by the de-mon;

Rubato
139
Slow Rubato
Chorale
Synth.
Vocal
Harm.
Piano
Bass
Drums
don't wan-na go by sa-tan, don't wan-na die un-ea-sy. Just let me go _ nat-'ral-ly. And when I die,

Fast 𝅗𝅥 = 126
Synth.
Vocal
and when I'm dead, dead and gone, There'll be one child born in our world to car-ry on, to car-ry on.
Harm.
Piano
Bass
Drums
A D D A
A D D A A D D A A D D A

AND WHEN I DIE

B♭ TENOR SAX

Words and Music by
LAURA NYRO

66
Slow "2" feel
D.S. al Coda
CODA
4
80
18
103
Slow "2" feel
8
111
Faster
10
121
Half Tempo Rock
4
Double Time
129
8
Rubato
Chorale - Slow Rubato
139
6
Fast
3

AND WHEN I DIE

1st B♭ TRUMPET

Words and Music by
LAURA NYRO

4
80
7
Slow "2" feel
103
8
111
Faster
10
121
Half Tempo Rock
3
Double Time
129
8
Rubato
Chorale - Slow Rubato
139
Fast
3

AND WHEN I DIE

2nd B♭ Trumpet

Words and Music by
LAURA NYRO

3
80
Slow "2" feel
8
103
Faster
111
10
121
Half Tempo Rock
3
Double Time
129
8
Rubato
139
Chorale - Slow Rubato
Fast
3

AND WHEN I DIE

TROMBONE

Words and Music by
LAURA NYRO

3
mf
103
Slow "2" feel
8
111
Faster
10
121
Half Tempo Rock
4
129
Double Time
8
Rubato
Chorale - Slow Rubato
139
Fast
3

GO DOWN GAMBLIN'

Words and Music by DAVID CLAYTON THOMAS
and FRED LIPSIUS

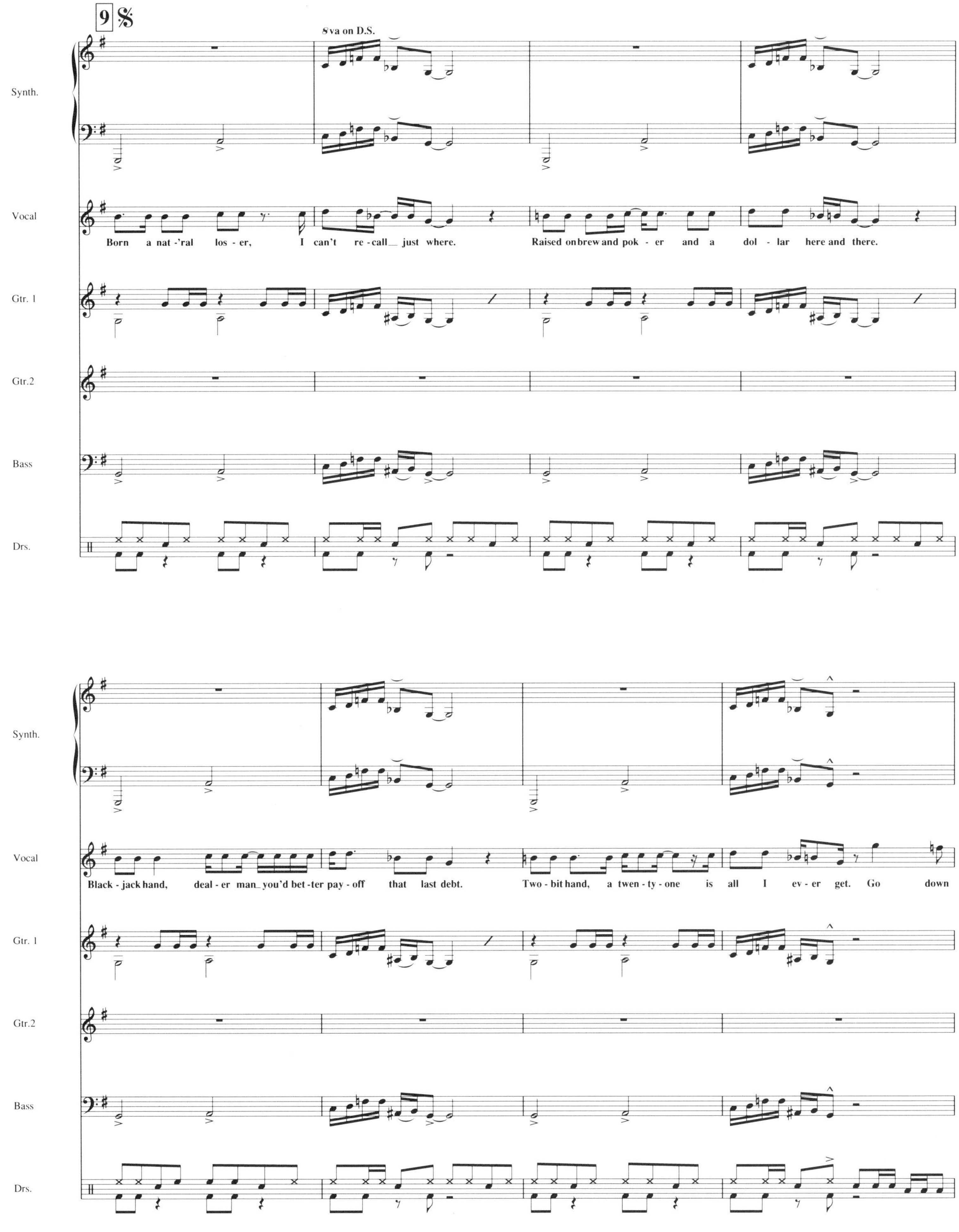
9
8va on D.S.
Synth.
Vocal
Born a nat-'ral los-er, I can't re-call just where.
Raised on brew and pok-er and a dol-lar here and there.
Gtr. 1
Gtr.2
Bass
Drs.
Synth.
Vocal
Black-jack hand, deal-er man you'd bet-ter pay-off that last debt.
Two-bit hand, a twen-ty-one is all I ev-er get. Go down
Gtr. 1
Gtr.2
Bass
Drs.

17
8va on D.S.
Synth.
Vocal
gam - blin,' say it when you're run - ning low, Go down
Gtr. 1
Gtr.2
C no3
Bass
Drs.
To Coda
gam - blin,' you may nev - er have to go, no.

Synth.
Vocal
Gtr. 1
Solo
Gtr.2
Bass
Drs.
29
Synth.
Vocal
Gtr. 1
Gtr.2
Bass
Drs.

Synth.
Vocal
Gtr. 1
Gtr.2
Bass
Drs.
37
Tambourine (drums tacet)

D.S. al Coda
Synth.
Vocal
Gtr. 1
Gtr.2
Bass
Drum Fill
Drs.

Coda
Synth.
Vocal
Solo
Gtr. 1
Gtr.2
G
Bass
Drs.

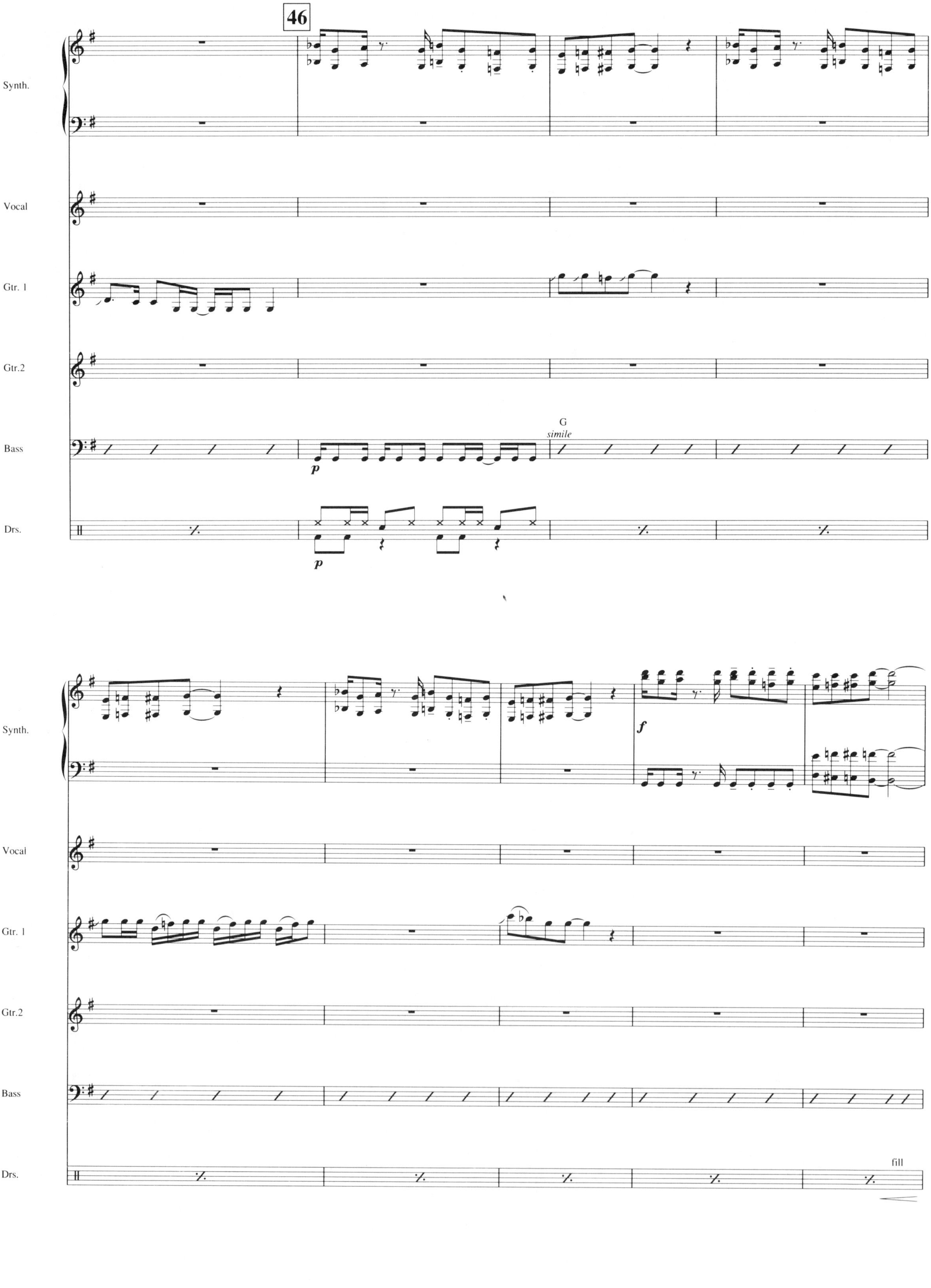
46
Synth.
Vocal
Gtr. 1
Gtr.2
Bass
Drs.
G
simile
p
p
f
Synth.
Vocal
Gtr. 1
Gtr.2
Bass
Drs.
fill

56
Synth.
Vocal
Gtr. 1
Gtr.2
Bass
Drs.
Solo 8va
(as played by David Clayton-Thomas)
ff
ff
ff
Synth.
Vocal
Gtr. 1
Gtr.2
Bass
Drs.

Synth.
Vocal
Gtr. 1
Gtr.2
Bass
Drs.
Synth.
Vocal
Gtr. 1
Gtr.2
Bass
Drs.

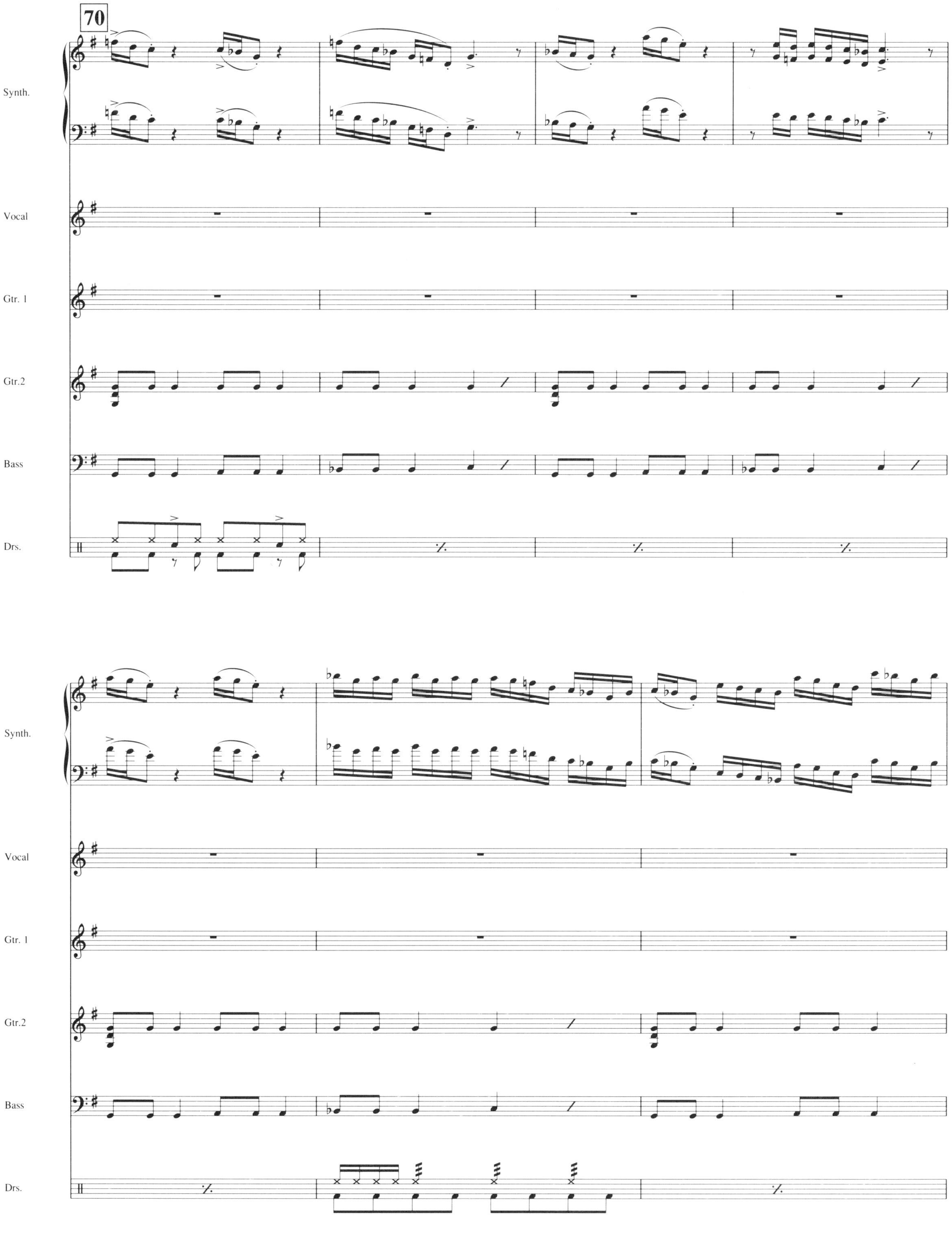
70
Synth.
Vocal
Gtr. 1
Gtr.2
Bass
Drs.

78
Synth.
Vocal
Go down gam - blin,' say it when you're run - ning low,
Gtr. 1
Gtr.2
G
(solo fill)
Bass
Drs.
Synth.
Vocal
Go down gam - blin,' you may nev - er have to go, no.
Gtr. 1
Gtr.2
G (solo fill)
Bass
Drs.

Synth.
Vocal
Go down gam - blin,' say it when you're run - ning low.
Gtr. 1
D
(fill)
Gtr.2
G
(solo fill)
Bass
Drs.
Synth.
Vocal
8va
Go down gam - blin,' you may nev - er have to go, no, no, no!
Gtr. 1
D
Gtr.2
G
Bass
Drs.

GO DOWN GAMBLIN'

Words and Music by DAVID CLAYTON THOMAS
and FRED LIPSIUS

B♭ SOPRANO SAX

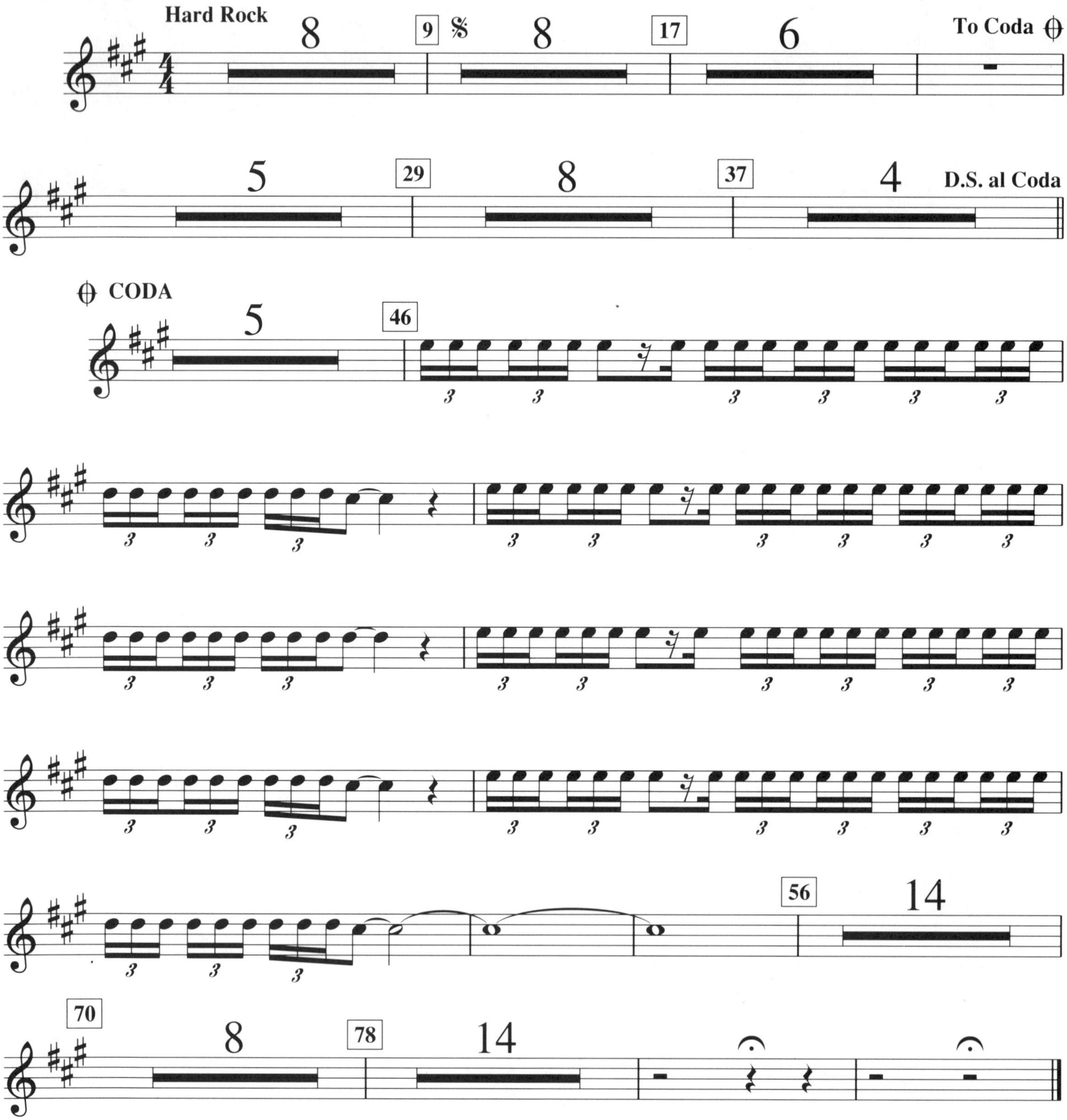

Piano

Go Down Gamblin'

32
3
3
3
3
35
3
D.S. al Coda
37
4
4
Coda
41
4
4
46
2
2
50
2
2
f
54
56
14
14
70

72
75
78
77
14
14

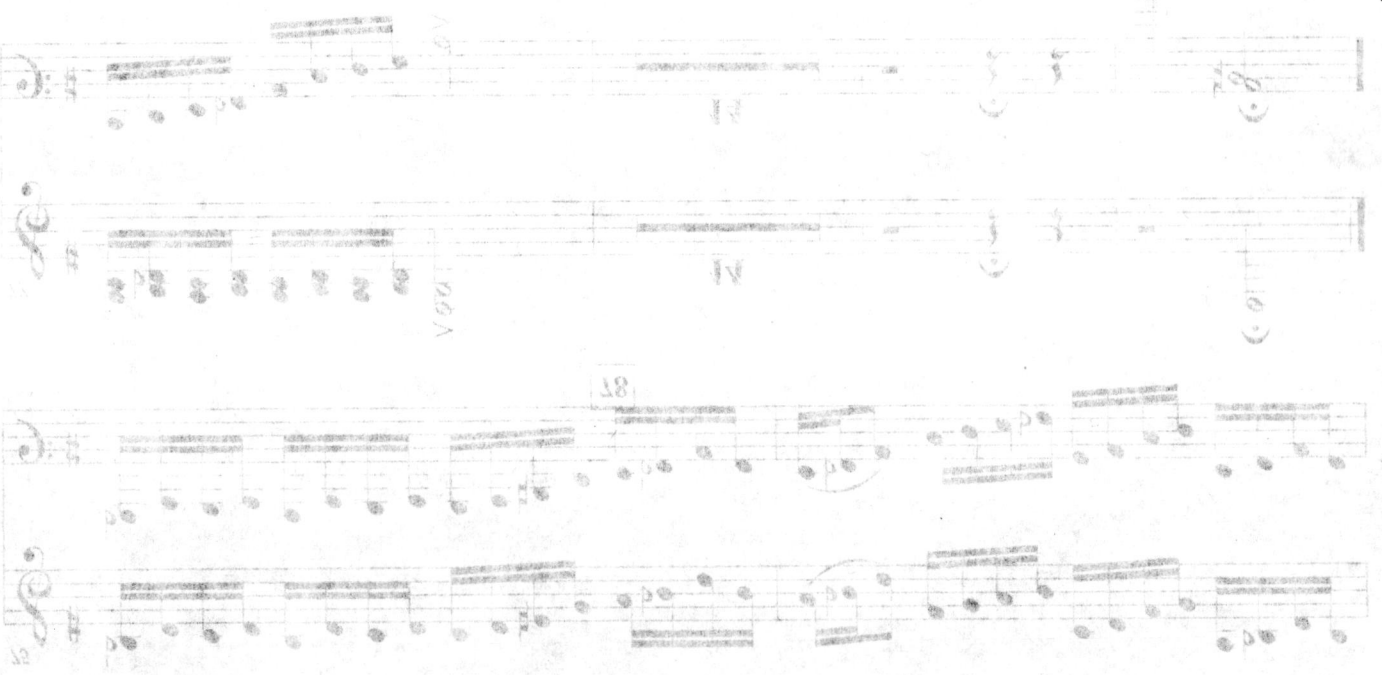

GO DOWN GAMBLIN'

B♭ TRUMPET 1

Words and Music by DAVID CLAYTON THOMAS
and FRED LIPSIUS

37
4
D.S. al Coda
CODA
8va
4
46
4
f
56
14
70
78
14

GO DOWN GAMBLIN'

B♭ TRUMPET 2

Words and Music by DAVID CLAYTON THOMAS
and FRED LIPSIUS

37
4
D.S. al Coda
CODA
4
46
56
14
70
78
14

GO DOWN GAMBLIN'

TROMBONE/TUBA

Words and Music by DAVID CLAYTON THOMAS
and FRED LIPSIUS

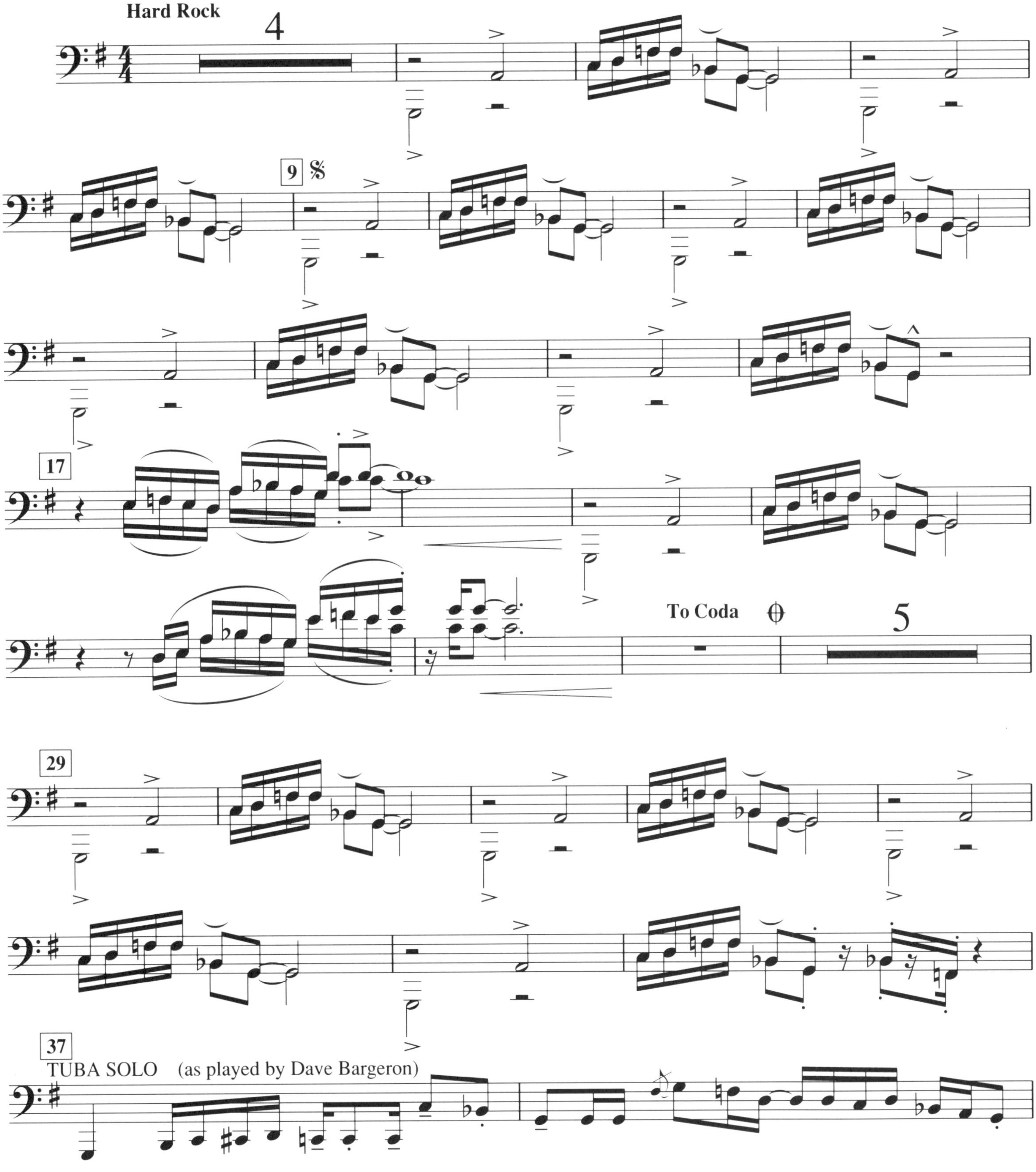

D.S. al Coda
CODA
4
46
p
f
56
14
70
Tuba - tacet
Add Tuba
78
14
Trombone
Tuba

GOD BLESS' THE CHILD

Words and Music by ARTHUR HERZOG JR.
and BILLIE HOLIDAY

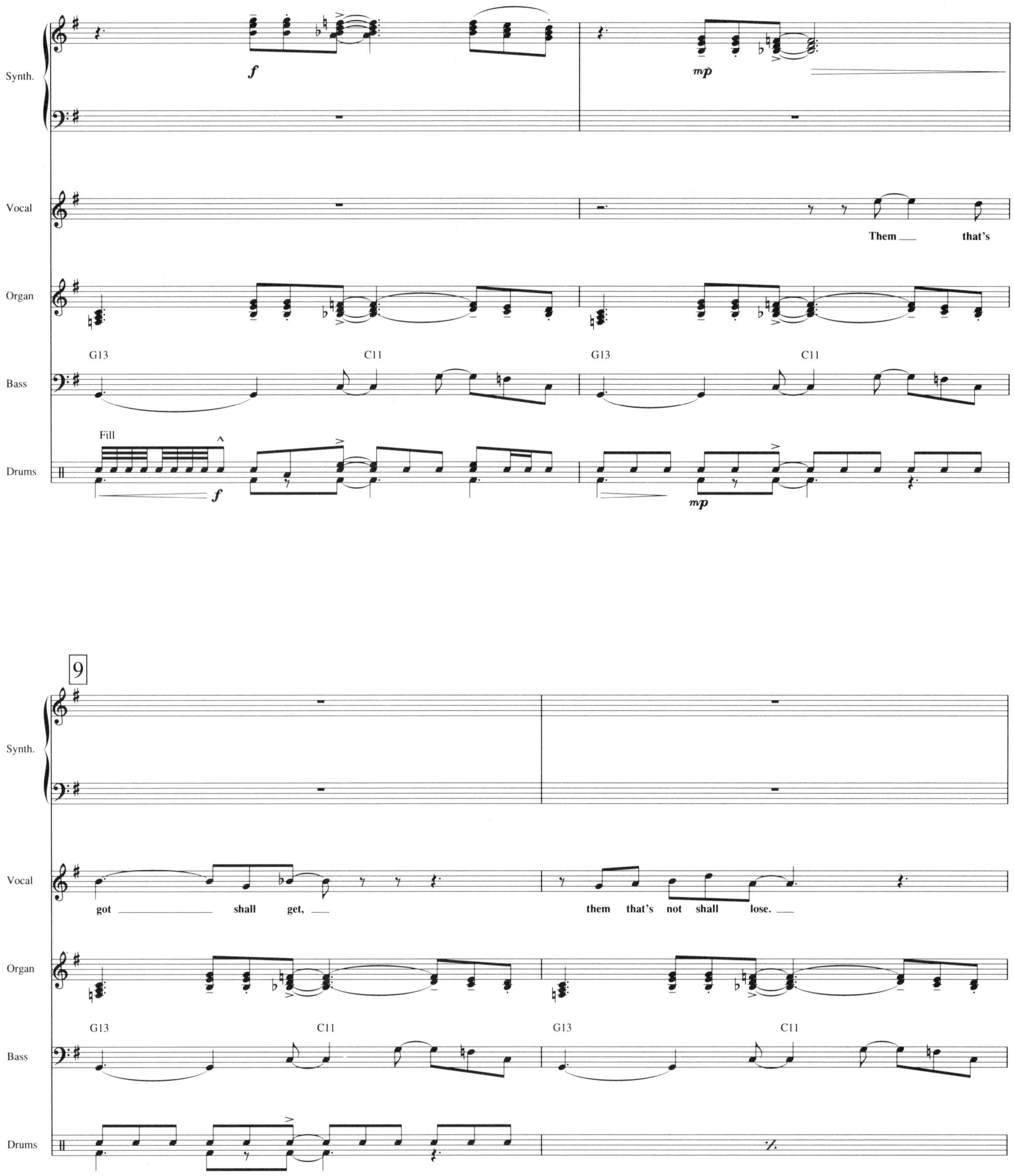
Synth.
Vocal
Organ
Bass
Drums
Fill
G13
C11
Them that's
9
got shall get,
them that's not shall lose.

Synth.
Vocal
So the Bi - ble says
and it still is news.
Organ
Dm/G
Dm(+7)
Dm7/G
G7(♭9)
Bass
Drums
Synth.
Vocal
Ma - ma may have
and pa - pa may have,
Organ
Cmaj7
F9(+11)
Bass
Drums

Synth.
Vocal
God bless the child that's got his own. Well that's got his
Organ
Bm7 E7 Am7 D7
Bass
Drums
Synth.
f
mp
Vocal
own. And the
Organ
G13 C11 G13 C11
Bass
Drums
f
mp

19
Synth.
Vocal
strong seem to get more,
while the weak ones fade;
Organ
G13 C11 G13 C11
Bass
Drums
Synth.
Vocal
emp - ty pock - ets don't
ev - er make the grade.
Organ
Bass
Drums

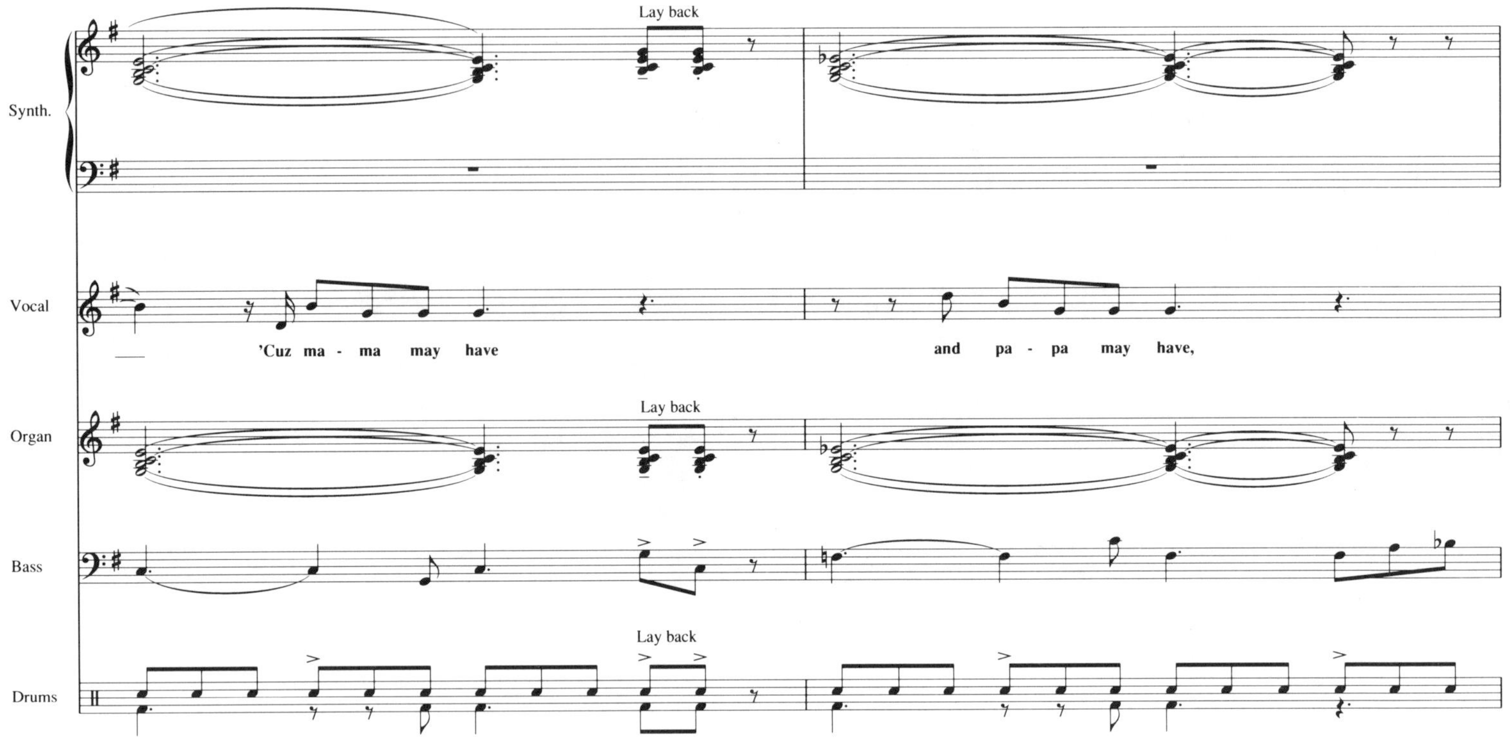
Lay back
Synth.
Vocal
'Cuz ma - ma may have
and pa - pa may have,
Organ
Lay back
Bass
Drums
Lay back

Synth.
Vocal
God bless the child that's got his own,
that's got his
Organ
Bass
Bm7
E7
Am7
D7
Drums

Synth.
Vocal
Organ
Bass
Drums
f
mp
own.
G13
C11
G13
C11
Bass sets tempo
With bass
f
mp
(4/4)
29
♩ = 72
Synth.
Vocal
Organ
Bass
Drums
And when ya got mon - ey,
ya got lots of friends _
Em
Em/D♯
Em/D
C7

Synth.
Vocal
crowd - in' 'round your door.
Organ
Bm Bm/A Gmaj7 Gmaj7/F♯
Bass
Drums
Fill
Synth.
Vocal
When the mon - ey's gone and all your spend - in' ends,
Organ
Em Em/D♯ Em/D C7
Bass
Drums

Synth.
rit.
rit.
Vocal
they won't be 'round any - y - more. No, no, no. And
rit.
Organ
Bass
Drums

38
♩. = 54
Synth.
Vocal
rich re - la - tions may give you a crust of bread and such.
Organ
G13
C11
G13
C11
Bass
Drums
p

Synth.
Vocal
You can help your - self
but don't take too much.
Organ
Dm/G
Dm(+7)
Dm/G
G7(♭9)
Bass
Drums
Lay back
Synth.
Vocal
Ma - ma may have
and pa - pa may have,
Lay back
Organ
Cmaj7
F9(+11)
Bass
Lay back
Drums

Synth.
Vocal
God bless the child that's got his own, that's got his own.
Organ
Bm7 E7 Am7 D7
Bass
Drums
𝅗𝅥 = 104 Bright Latin feel
Synth.
Vocal
Acoustic Piano 8 va basso
Organ
Bass
Drums

51
Synth.
Vocal
Organ
Bass
(+Drums)
(fills)
Drums

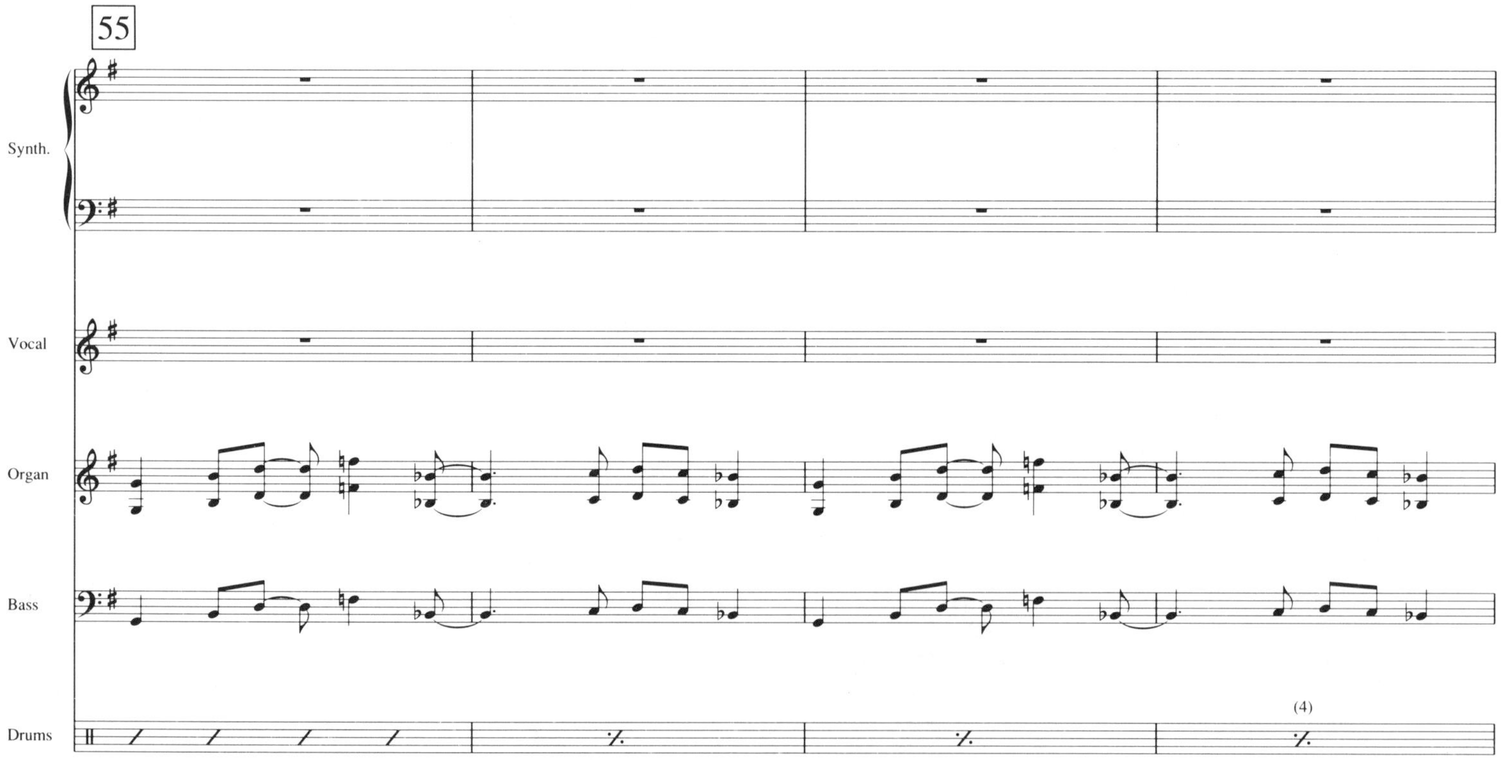
55
Synth.
Vocal
Organ
Bass
Drums
(4)

Synth.
Vocal
Organ
Bass
(8)
Drums

Synth.
Vocal
Organ
Bass
2
Drums

Synth.
Vocal
Organ
Bass
Drums
2
71
Synth.
Vocal
Organ
Bass
Drums
(4)

Synth.
Vocal
Organ
Bass
G13
Drums
79
Jazz 4
Synth.
Vocal
Organ
Cmaj7
F13
Bass
(4)
Drums

Synth.
Vocal
Organ
Bm7
E7(+9)
Am7
D7(+9)
Bass
Drums
Fill
(4)

87
Latin
Synth.
Vocal
Organ
Bass
Drums
(4)

Synth.
Vocal
Organ
Bass
Drums
1
2
111
In 4 - Majestically
♩=80
Synth.
Vocal
And when ya got mon - ey,
ya got lots of friends _
Organ
ff
Organ
Bass
f
Drums

Synth.
Vocal
they're crowd - in' 'round your door. But wait a min- ute child - ren,
Organ
Bass
Drums
f
Synth.
Vocal
when the mon - ey's gone and all your spend - ing ends
Organ
Bass
Drums

Rubato
Synth.
Vocal
they won't be 'round an - y - more.
No, no.
And
Organ solo - no bass
Organ
Bass - tacet
Bass
rit.
Drums
120
Slow Gospel feel ♩. = 54
rich re - la - tions may give you
a crust of bread and such
G13
C11
G13
C11

Synth.
Vocal
you can help your - self
but don't take too much.
Organ
Dm/G
Dm(+7)
Dm7/G
G7(♭9)
Bass
Drums

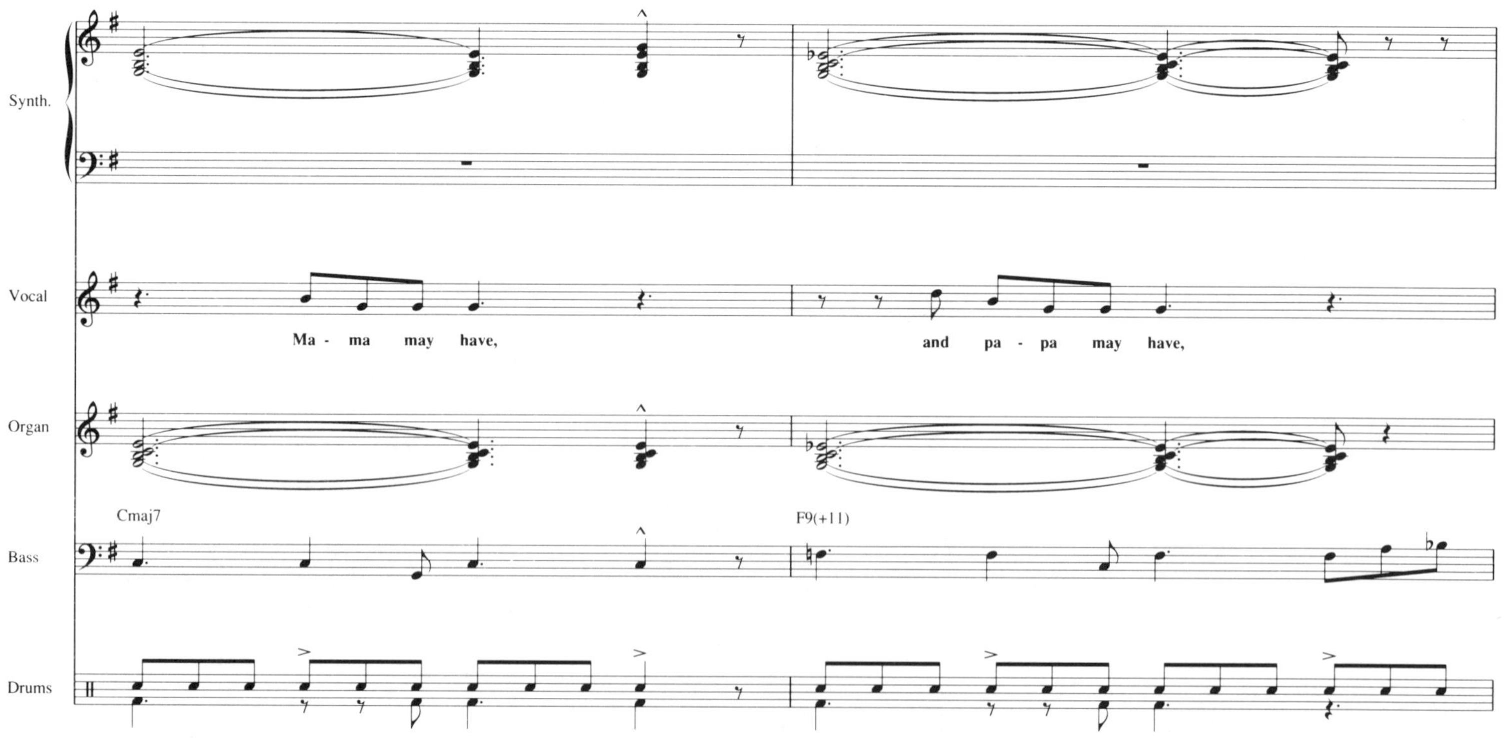
Synth.
Vocal
Ma - ma may have,
and pa - pa may have,
Organ
Cmaj7
F9(+11)
Bass
Drums

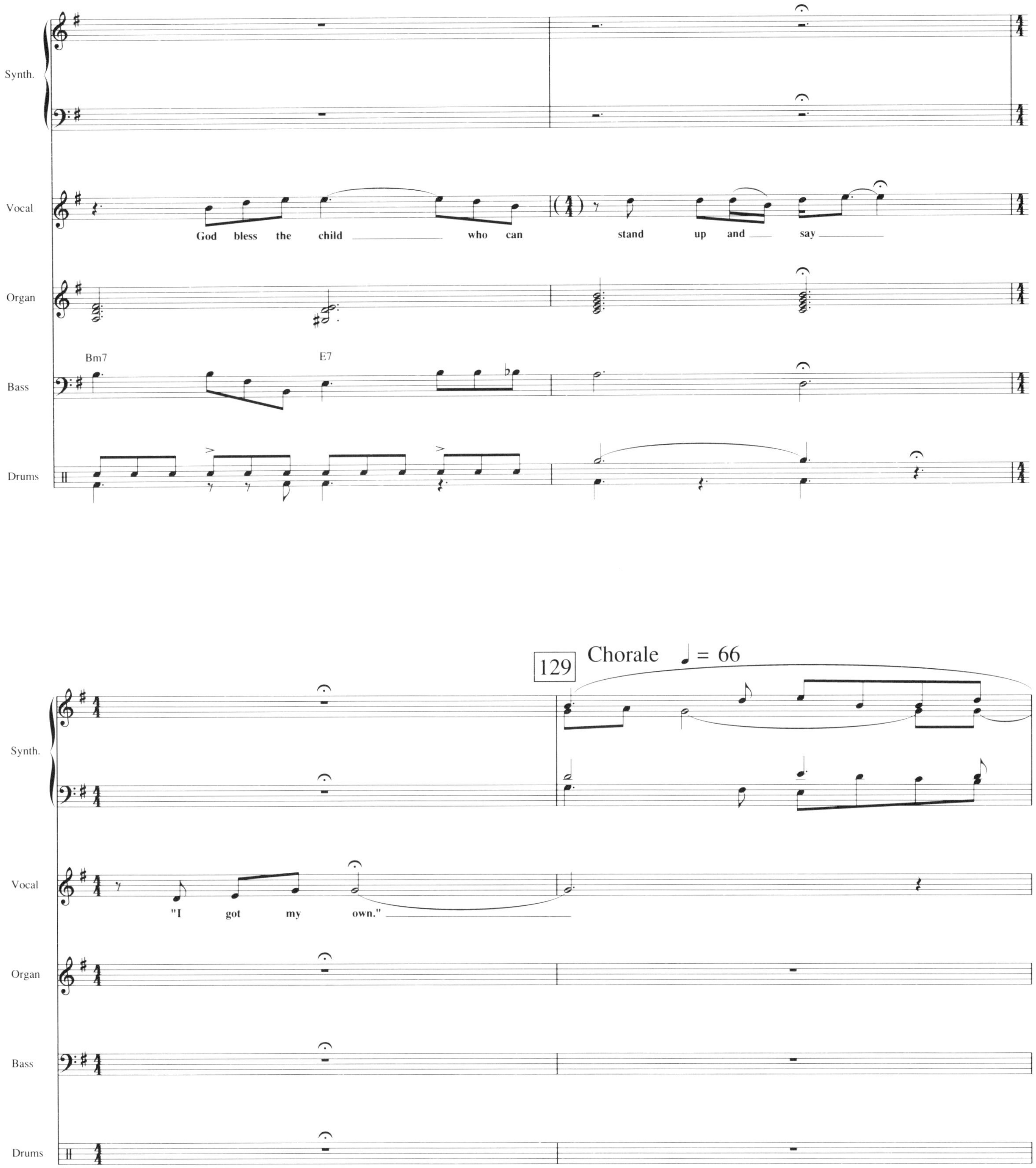
Synth.
Vocal
God bless the child who can stand up and say
Organ
Bm7
E7
Bass
Drums
129
Chorale ♩ = 66
Synth.
Vocal
"I got my own."
Organ
Bass
Drums

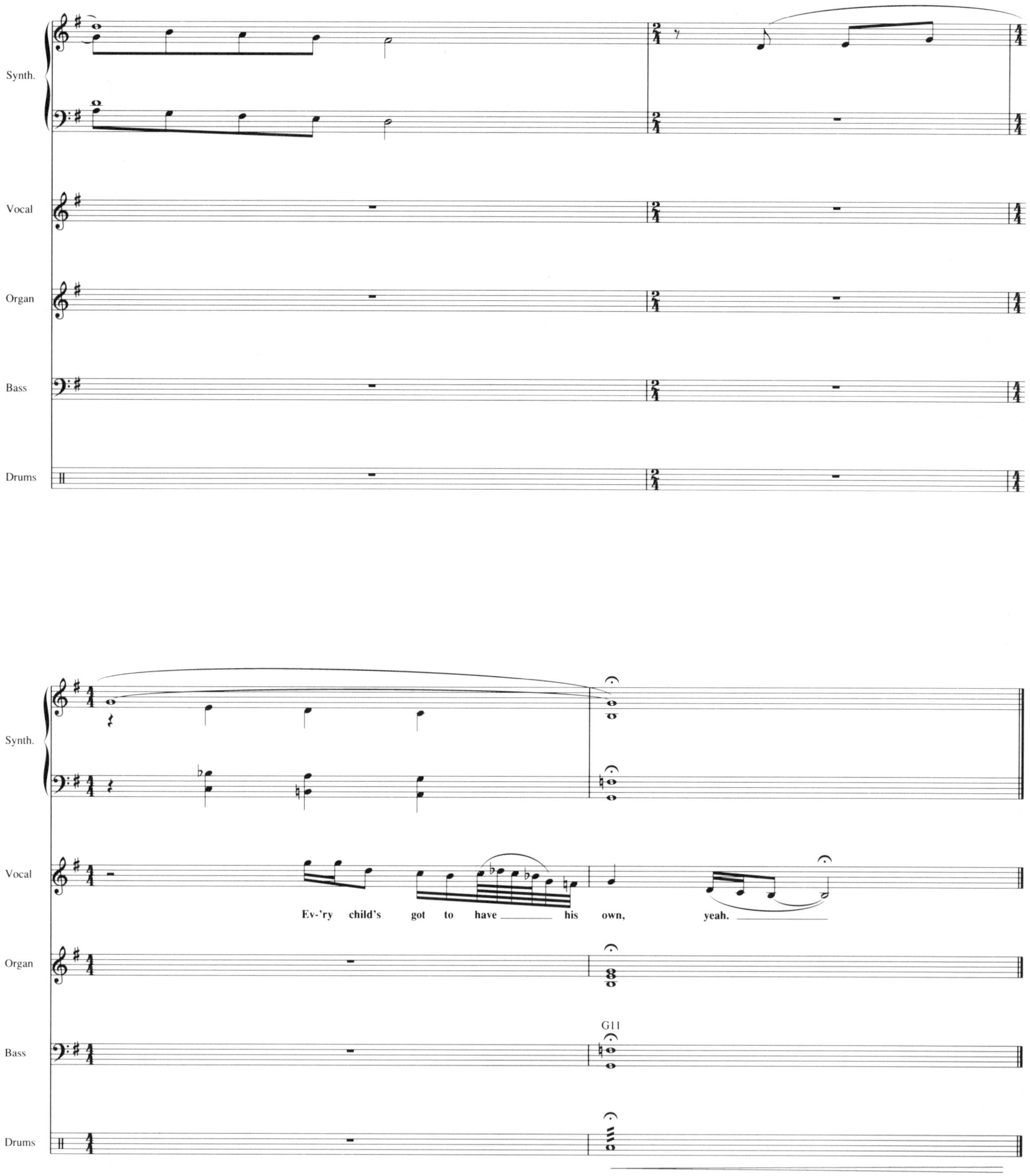
Synth.
Vocal
Organ
Bass
Drums
Synth.
Vocal
Ev-'ry child's got to have his own, yeah.
Organ
G11
Bass
Drums

GOD BLESS' THE CHILD

HARMONICA

Words and Music by ARTHUR HERZOG JR.
and BILLIE HOLIDAY

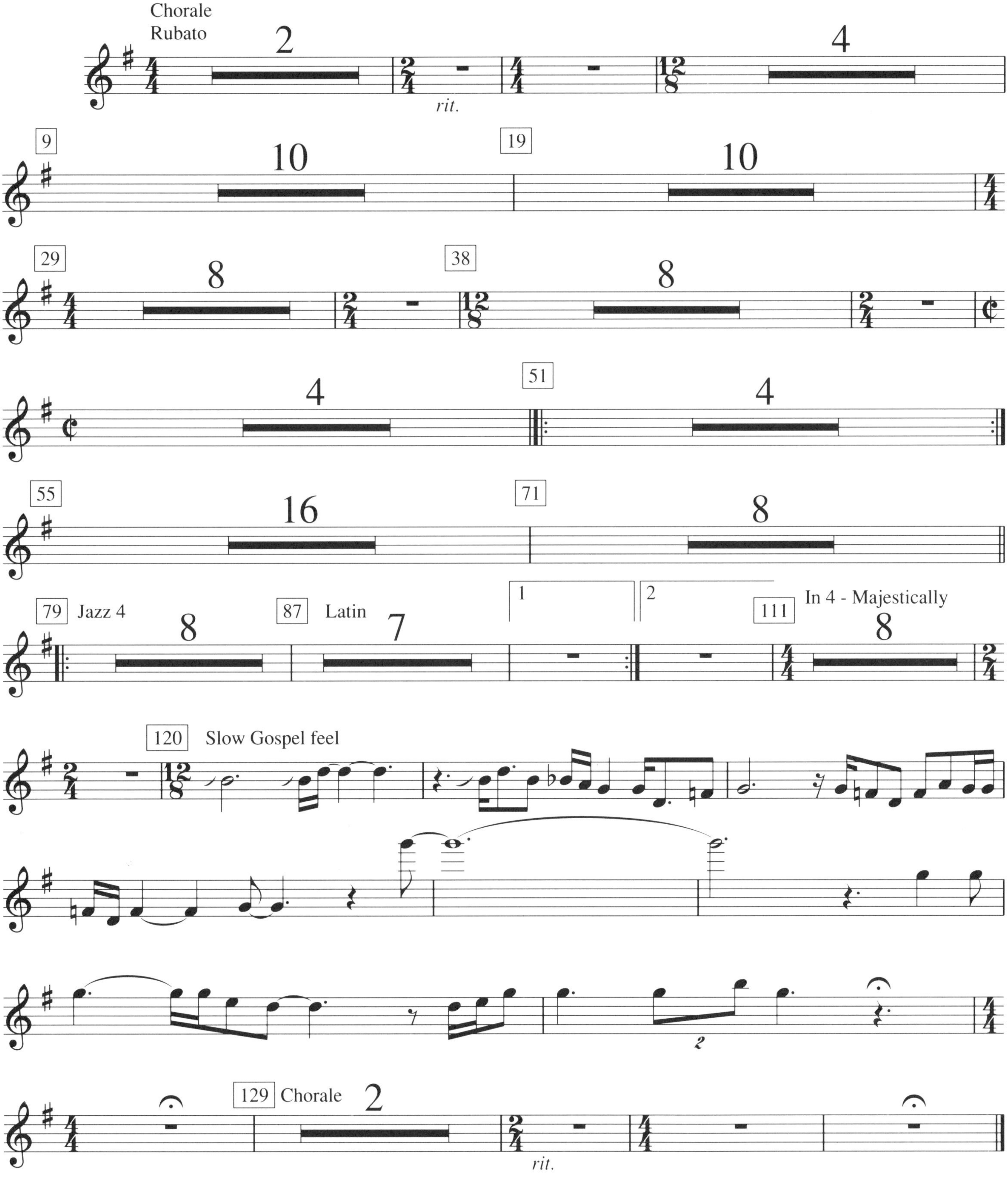

GOD BLESS' THE CHILD

B♭ TENOR SAX

Words and Music by ARTHUR HERZOG JR.
and BILLIE HOLIDAY

2
Bright Latin feel
4
51
shake
55
16
71
To Alto Sax
7
Amaj7
Solo 2nd x
as played by Fred Lipsius
D7
G♯m7
C♯7(+9)
F♯m7
B7+9
87
Play both x's
1
2
111
To Tenor
7
120
2
129
rit.

GOD BLESS' THE CHILD

1st B♭ TRUMPET

Words and Music by ARTHUR HERZOG JR. and BILLIE HOLIDAY

Chorale
Rubato

51
shake
55
16
71
4
1st x solo - as played by Lew Soloff
79
Jazz 4
Dmaj7
G13
C♯m7
F♯7(+4)
Bm7
E7(+9)
87
Play both times
Latin
Optional improvisations over figure
1
2
111
In 4 - Majestically
3
Rubato
2
120
Slow Gospel feel
2
129
Chorale
rit.

GOD BLESS' THE CHILD

2nd B♭ TRUMPET

Words and Music by ARTHUR HERZOG JR.
and BILLIE HOLIDAY

51
f
shake
55
16
71
Solo
3
79
Jazz 4
6
Play both x's
Optional improvisations over figure
1
2
In 4 - Majestically
3
f
Rubato
2
120
Slow Gospel feel
2
p
129
Chorale
mf
rit.

GOD BLESS' THE CHILD

TROMBONE

Words and Music by ARTHUR HERZOG JR.
and BILLIE HOLIDAY

51
Solo - as played by Jerry Hyman
55
8 va
71
79
Jazz 4
Latin
In 4 - Majestically
Rubato
120
Slow Gospel feel
rit.

LUCRETIA MAC EVIL

Words and Music by
DAVID CLAYTON THOMAS

R.H. 2nd x
L.H. 1st x
Syn./Hns.
Vocal
game?
Hard luck and trou - ble
Guitar
Piano/Org.
E7+9
A7sus
F♯13
B7+9
Bass
Drums
bound to be your claim to fame.

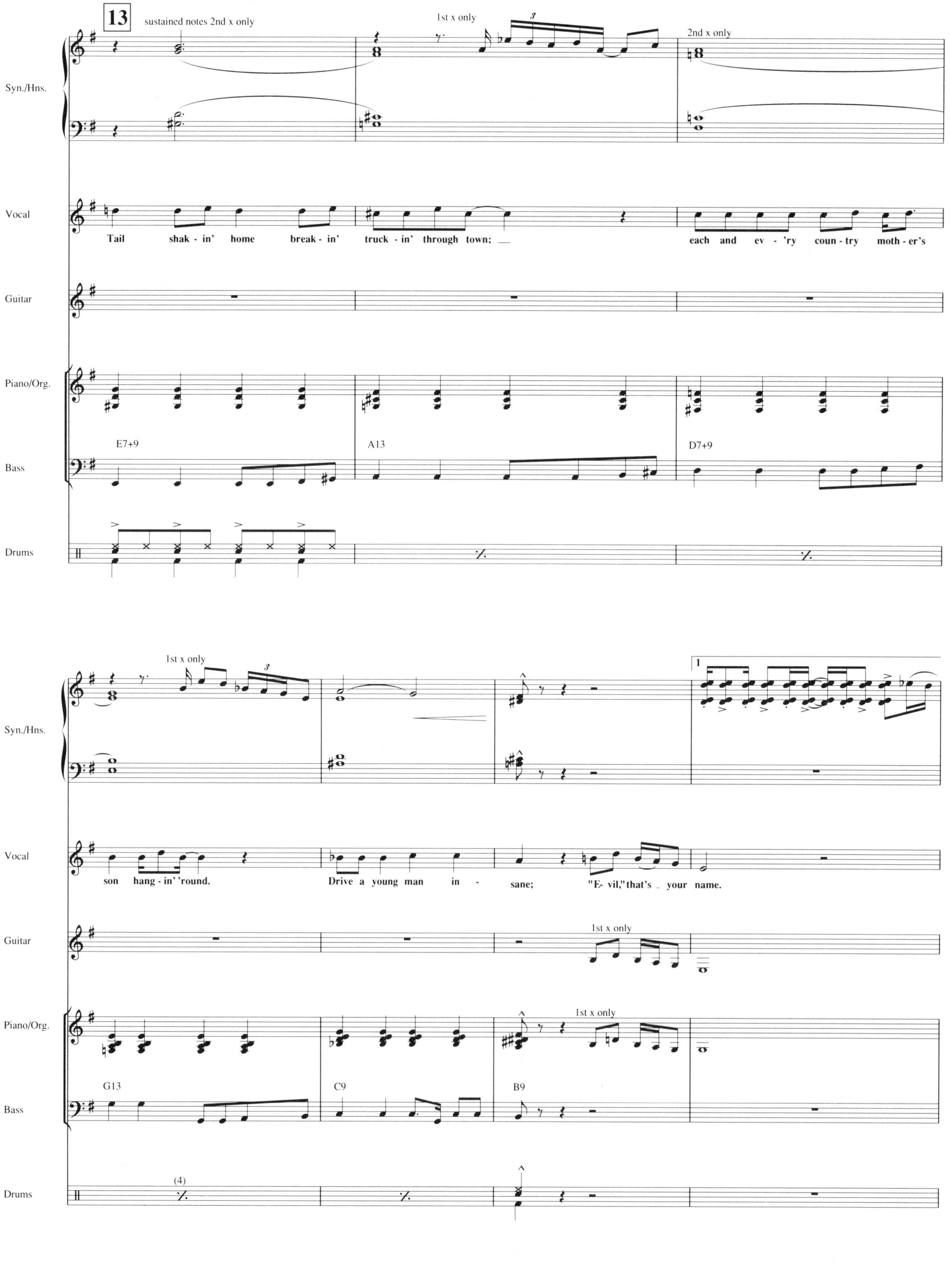
13
sustained notes 2nd x only
1st x only
2nd x only
Syn./Hns.
Vocal
Tail shak-in' home break-in' truck-in' through town; each and ev-'ry coun-try moth-er's
Guitar
Piano/Org.
E7+9
A13
D7+9
Bass
Drums
1st x only
1
son hang-in' 'round. Drive a young man in-sane; "E-vil," that's your name.
1st x only
1st x only
G13
C9
B9
(4)

Syn./Hns.
Vocal
Guitar
Piano/Org.
Bass
Drums
(spoken)
Talk a-bout it
2. Lu-
E7+9
A7sus
F♯13
B7+9
2
25
child.
Dev- il got you; Lu - cy; un - der lock and key,
TO ORGAN - AD LIB SINISTER " COUNT DRACULA" SOUNDS
E7+9

Syn./Hns.
Vocal
ain't a - bout to set you free.
Signed, sealed and wit - nessed on the day you were born.
Guitar
Piano/Org.
Bass
Drums
Rit.
A Tempo
a tempo
No use tryin' to fake him out, no use tryin' to make him out, soon he'll be tak- ing out his due.
What you goin' to do? Ooh!
(8)
To Piano
Em
Bsus

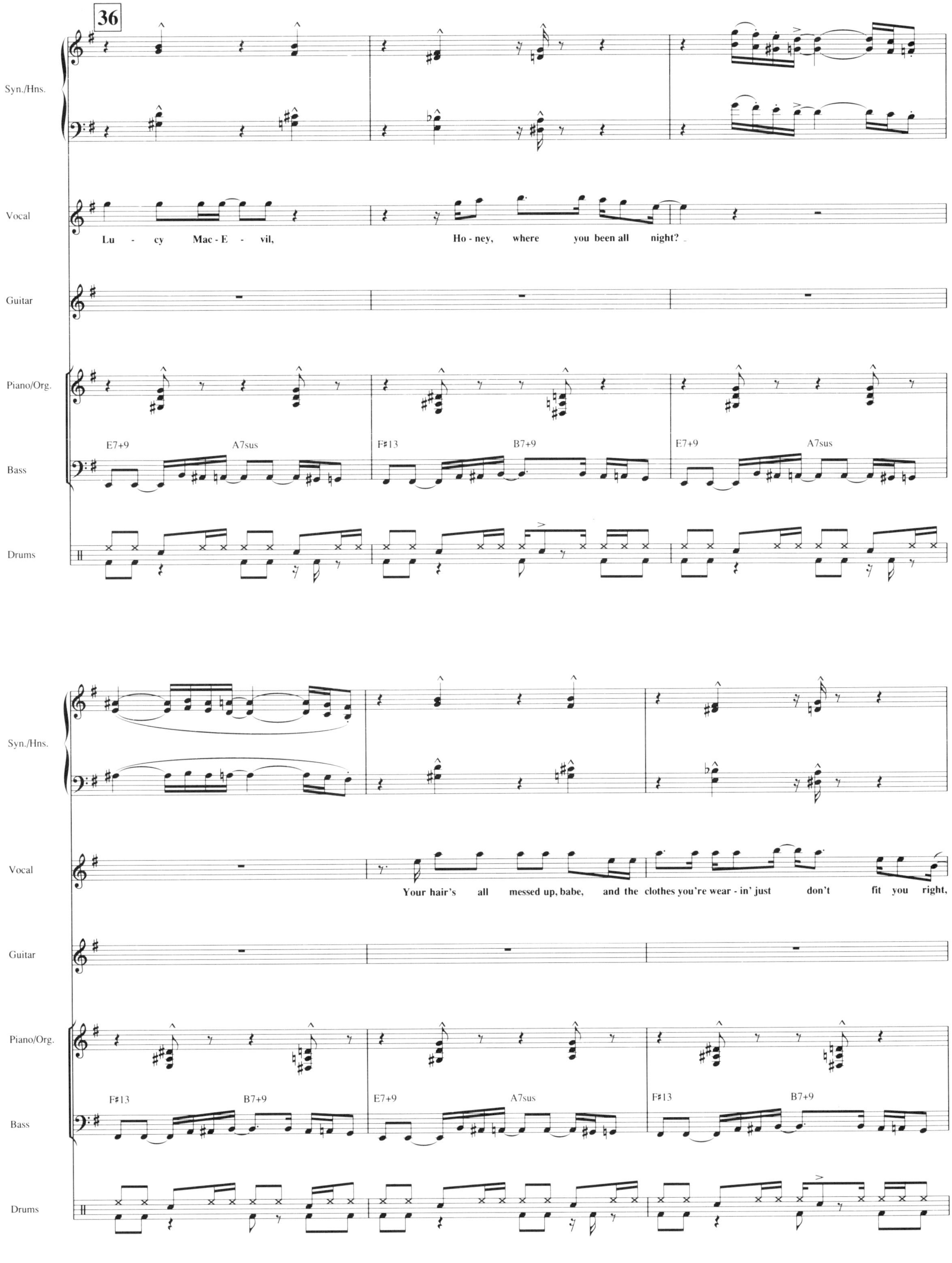
36
Syn./Hns.
Vocal
Lu - cy Mac - E - vil,
Ho - ney, where you been all night?
Guitar
Piano/Org.
E7+9
A7sus
F♯13
B7+9
E7+9
A7sus
Bass
Drums
Syn./Hns.
Vocal
Your hair's all messed up, babe, and the clothes you're wear - in' just don't fit you right,
Guitar
Piano/Org.
F♯13
B7+9
E7+9
A7sus
F♯13
B7+9
Bass
Drums

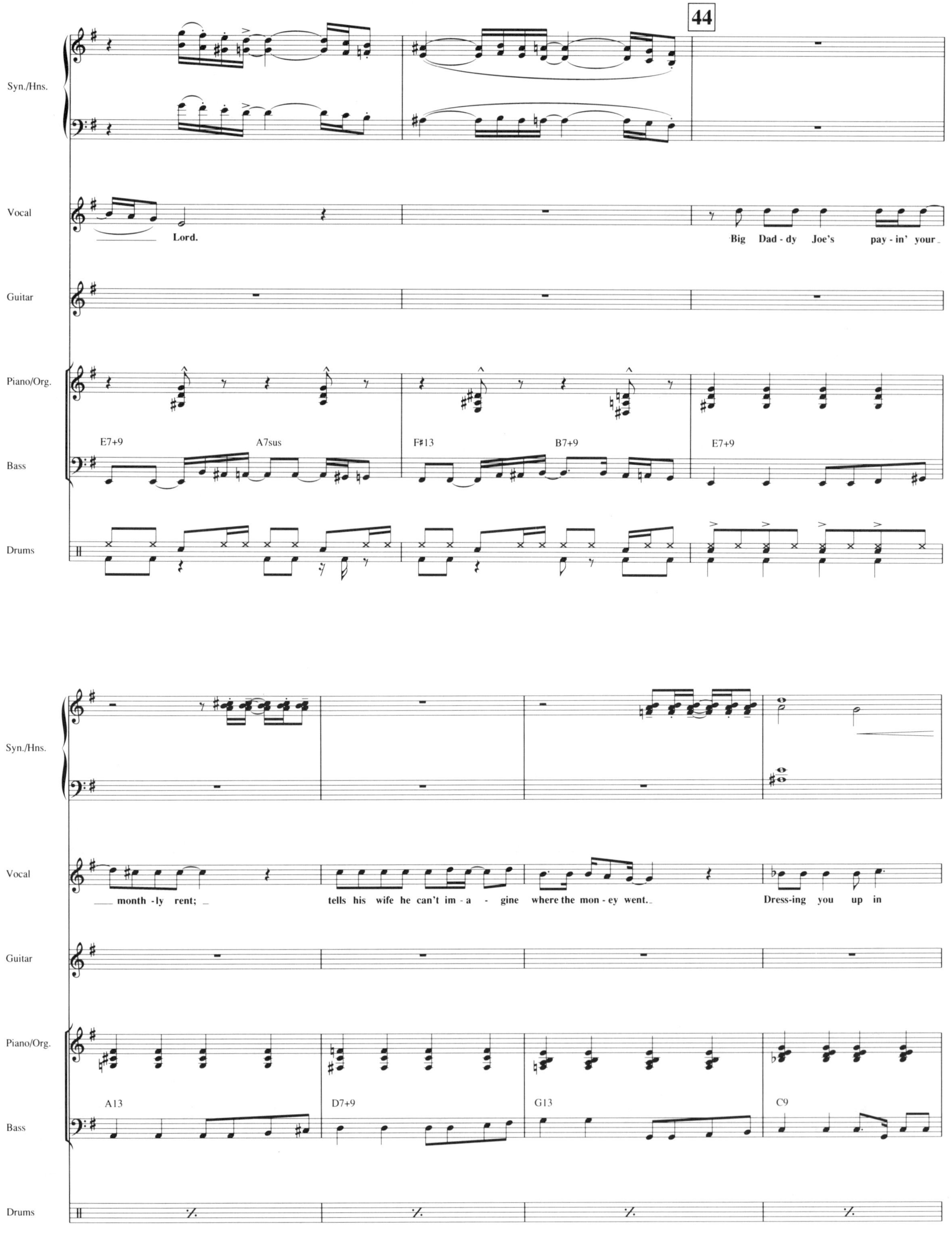

44
Syn./Hns.
Vocal
Lord.
Big Dad - dy Joe's pay - in' your
Guitar
Piano/Org.
E7+9
A7sus
F♯13
B7+9
E7+9
Bass
Drums
Syn./Hns.
Vocal
month - ly rent;
tells his wife he can't im - a - gine
where the mon - ey went.
Dress - ing you up in
Guitar
Piano/Org.
A13
D7+9
G13
C9
Bass
Drums

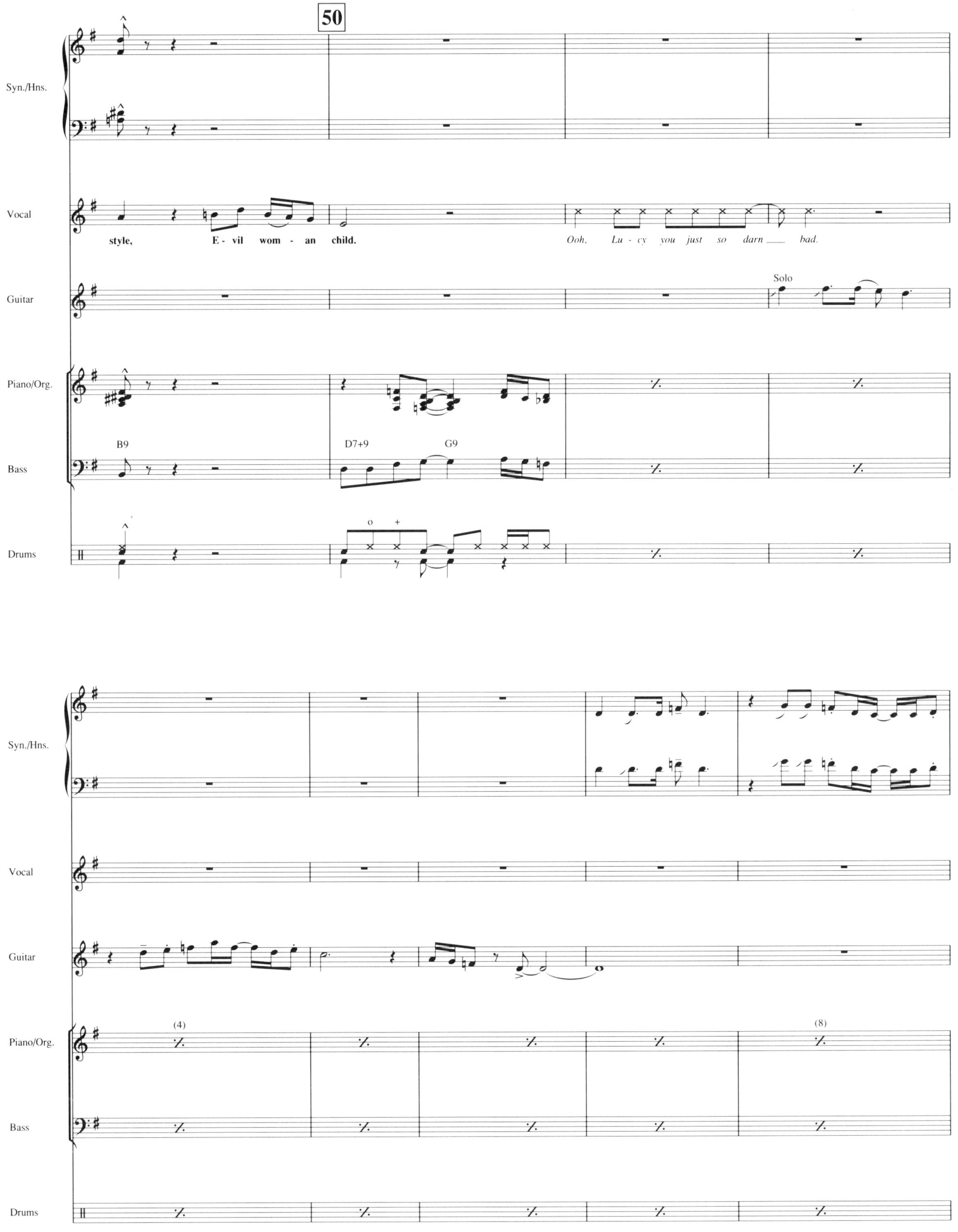
50
Syn./Hns.
Vocal
style, E - vil wom - an child.
Ooh, Lu - cy you just so darn bad.
Guitar
Solo
Piano/Org.
B9
D7+9
G9
Bass
Drums
Syn./Hns.
Vocal
Guitar
Piano/Org.
(4)
(8)
Bass
Drums

60
Syn./Hns.
Vocal
Guitar
Piano/Org.
(4)
Eb7+9
Ab9
Eb7+9
Ab9
Bass
Drums

Syn./Hns.
Vocal
Guitar
Piano/Org.
Bass
Drums

LUCRETIA MAC EVIL

E♭ ALTO SAXOPHONE

Words and Music by
DAVID CLAYTON THOMAS

rit.
a tempo
36
2
2
44
50
10
60
7

LUCRETIA MAC EVIL

B♭ TRUMPET 1

Words and Music by
DAVID CLAYTON THOMAS

rit.
a tempo
36
6
44
50
10
60

LUCRETIA MAC EVIL

B♭ TRUMPET 2

Words and Music by
DAVID CLAYTON THOMAS

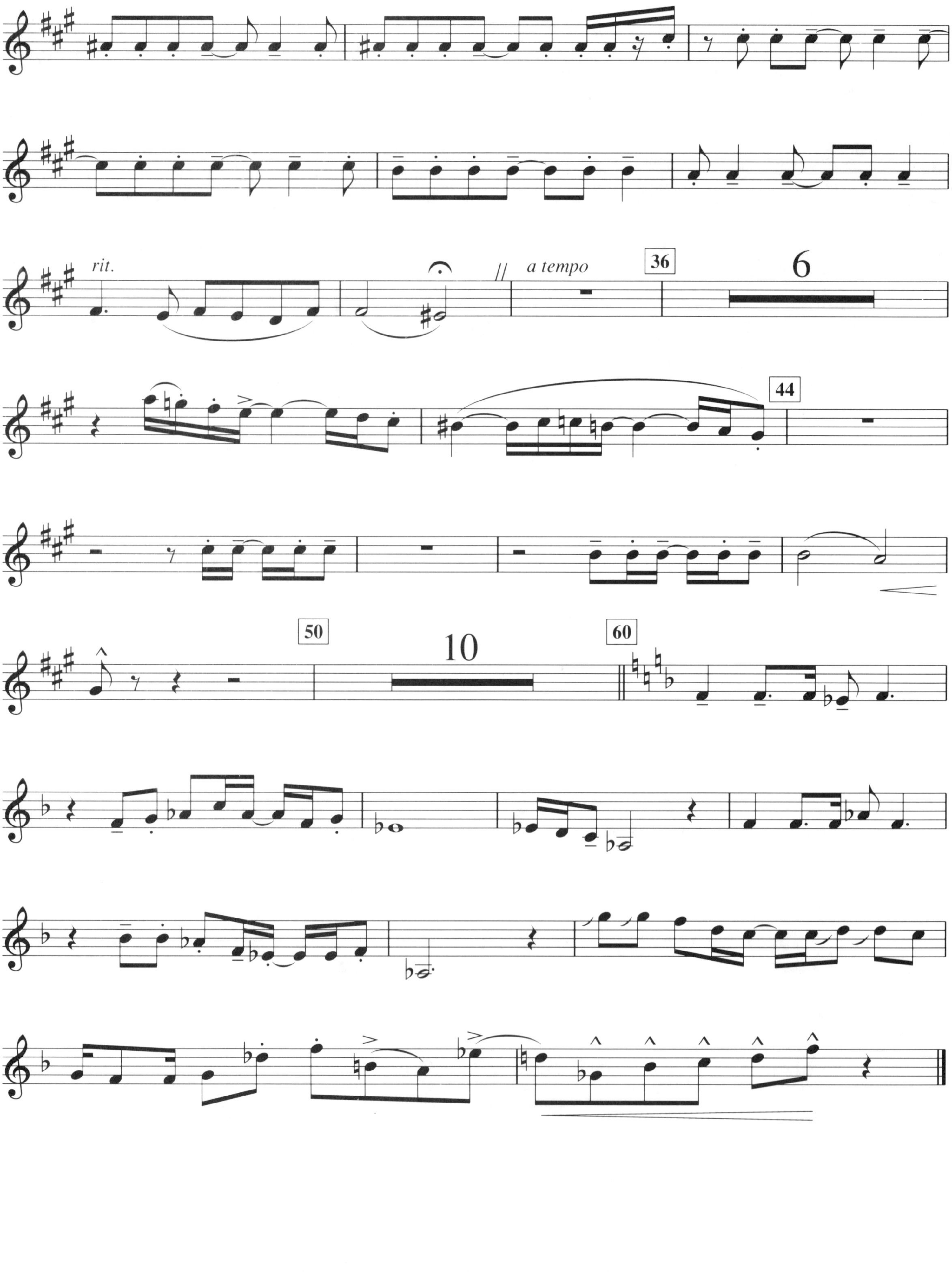
rit.
a tempo
36
6
44
50
10
60

LUCRETIA MAC EVIL

TROMBONE

Words and Music by
DAVID CLAYTON THOMAS

rit.
a tempo
36
2
2
4
44
50
6
60

SOMETIMES IN WINTER

Words and Music by
STEVEN KATZ

Ballad ♩ = 80

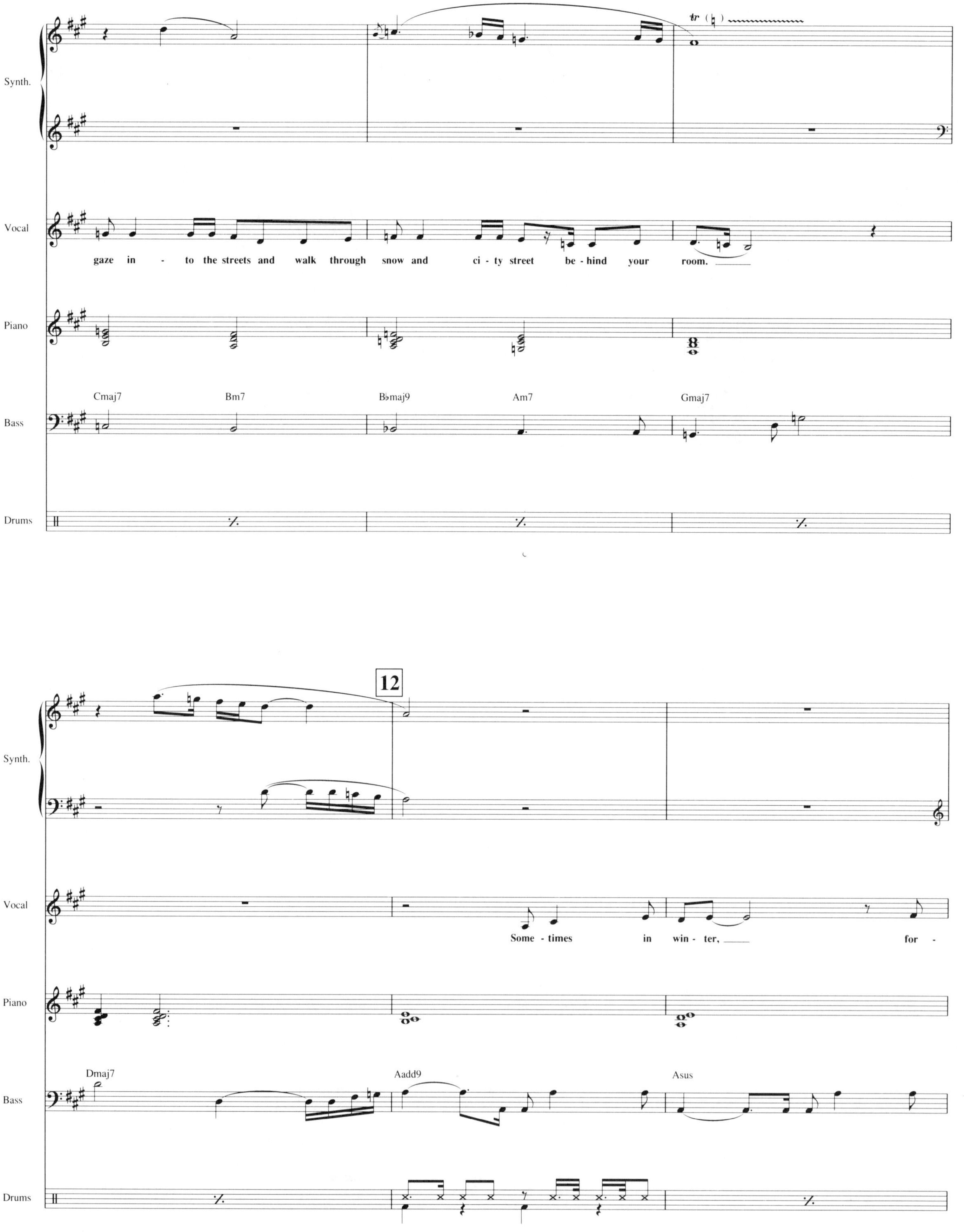
Synth.
Vocal
gaze in - to the streets and walk through snow and ci - ty street be - hind your room.
Piano
Cmaj7 Bm7 B♭maj9 Am7 Gmaj7
Bass
Drums
12
Synth.
Vocal
Some - times in win - ter, for -
Piano
Dmaj7 Aadd9 Asus
Bass
Drums

Synth.
Vocal
got - ten mem- o- ries re - mem - ber you be - hind the trees with leaves that cried.
Piano
Cmaj7 Bm7 B♭maj9 Am7 Gmaj7
Bass
Drums
Synth.
Vocal
Piano
Dmaj7 Aadd9
Bass
Drums

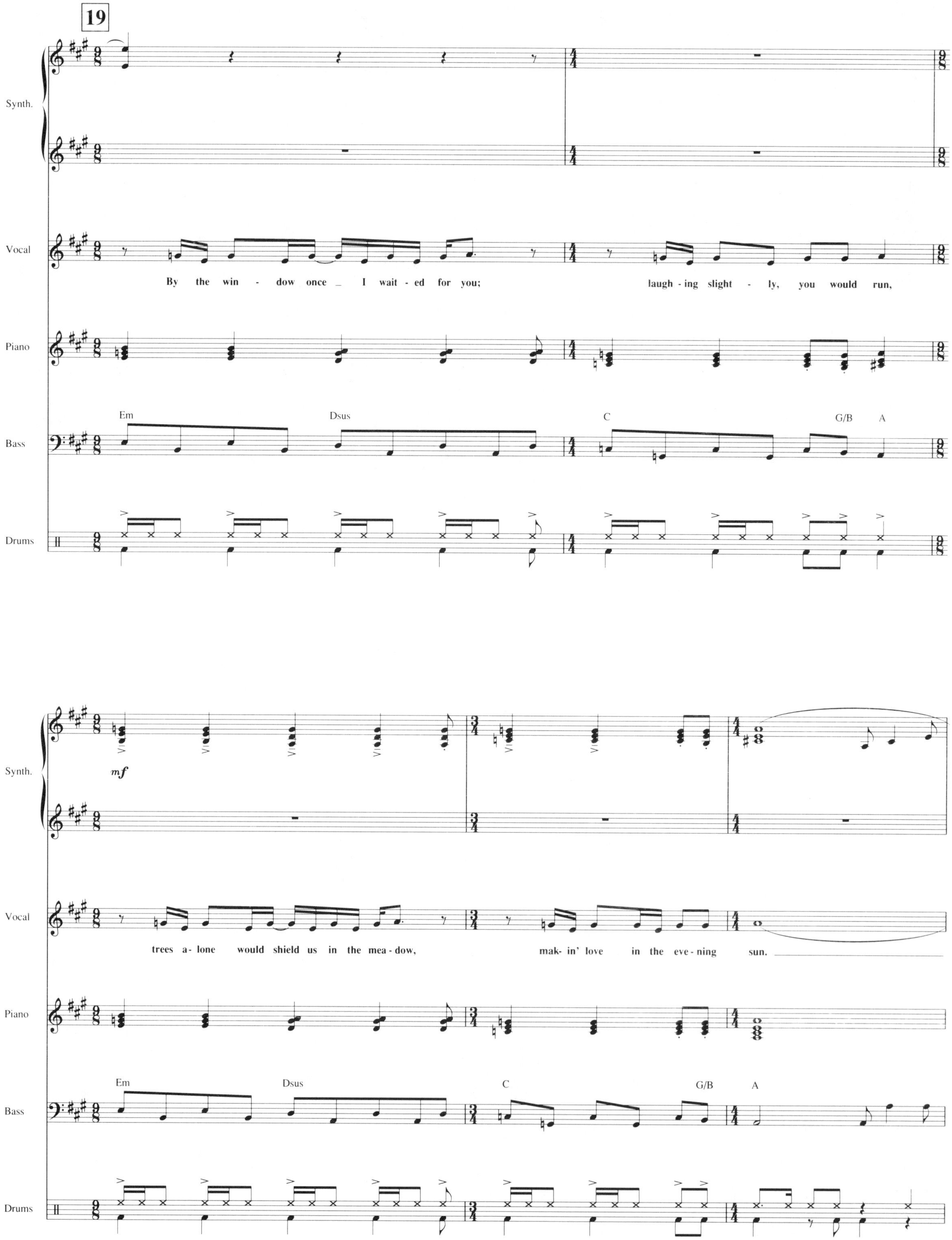
19
Synth.
Vocal
By the win - dow once _ I wait - ed for you;
laugh - ing slight - ly, you would run,
Piano
Em
Dsus
C
G/B
A
Bass
Drums
mf
trees a - lone would shield us in the mea - dow,
mak - in' love in the eve - ning sun.

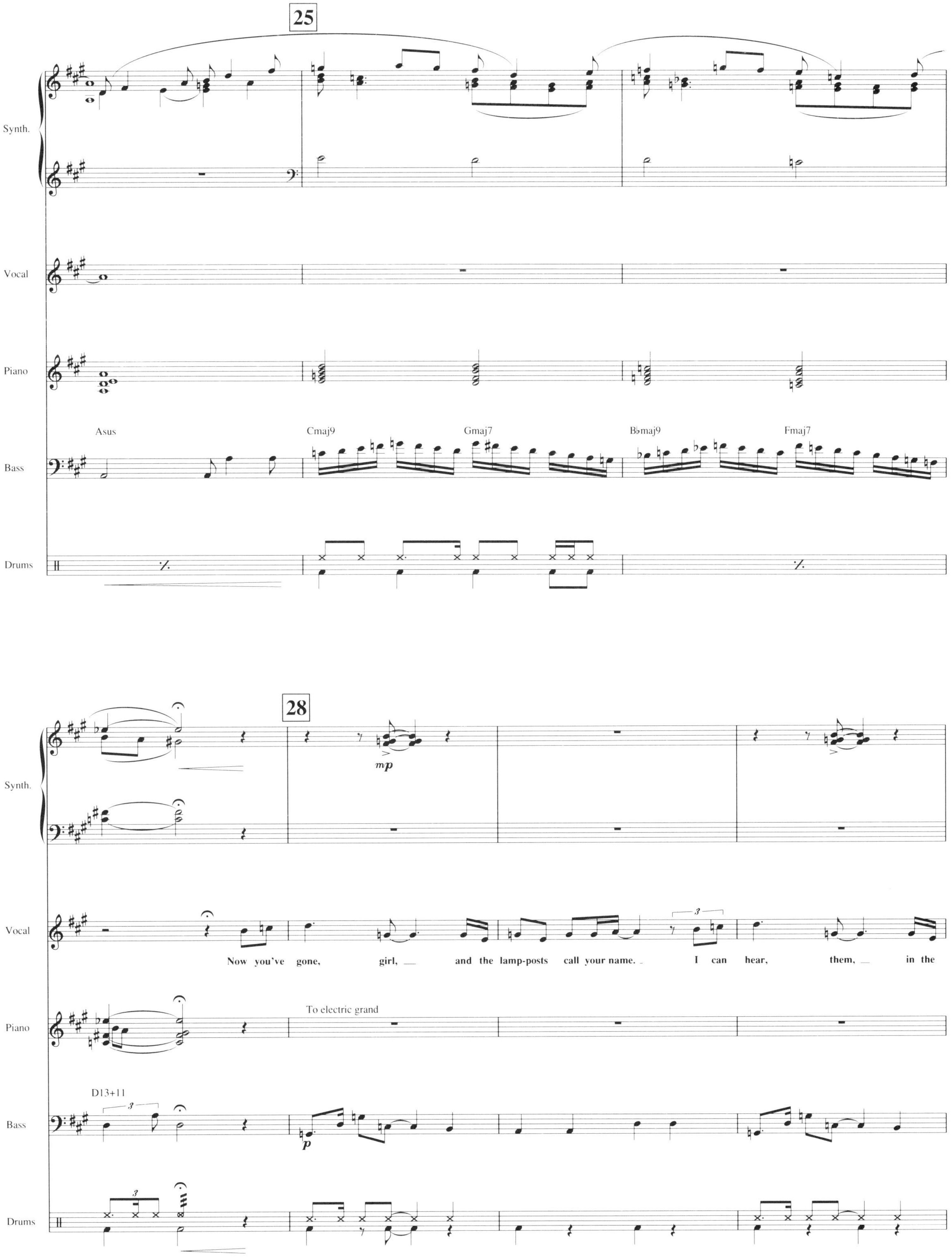
25
Synth.
Vocal
Piano
Asus
Cmaj9
Gmaj7
B♭maj9
Fmaj7
Bass
Drums
28
mp
Now you've gone, girl, — and the lamp-posts call your name. _ I can hear, them, — in the
To electric grand
D13+11
p

Synth.
p
Vocal
spring of fro- zen rain. Now you've gone, girl, and the times slow down till dawn, it's a cold room and the walls ask where you've
Piano
Electric grand
Bass
Bm Em C
Drums
To sticks
Synth.
Vocal
gone.
Piano
Aadd9 Asus Aadd9 Asus
8va
Bass
mf
Jazz feel
Drums
mf

40
Synth.
Vocal
Piano
Aadd9
Asus
Aadd9
Bass
Drums
Synth.
Vocal
Piano
Asus
Aadd9
Asus
Bass
Drums

48
Synth.
Vocal
Piano
Bass
Drums
Some - times in
Aadd9
Asus
Aadd9
loco
To brushes
win - ter, I love you when the good times seem like mem- 'ries in the spring that nev - er
Asus
Cmaj7
Bm7
B♭maj9
Am7

Synth.
Vocal
Piano
Bass
Drums
tr
54
came.
Some - times in
Gmaj7
Dmaj7
Aadd9
win - ter,
I
wish the
emp - ty
streets would fill
with
laugh - ter
from your tears
to ease my
Asus
Cmaj7
Bm7
B♭maj9
Am7

Synth.
Vocal
pain.
Piano
Bass
Drums
Bm
Cmaj7
8va
Gmaj7

Synth.
Vocal
Piano
Solo
Bass
Drums
B♭maj7
Fmaj7
loco
Bm
Em/G

SOMETIMES IN WINTER

FLUTE/TENOR SAX

Words and Music by
STEVEN KATZ

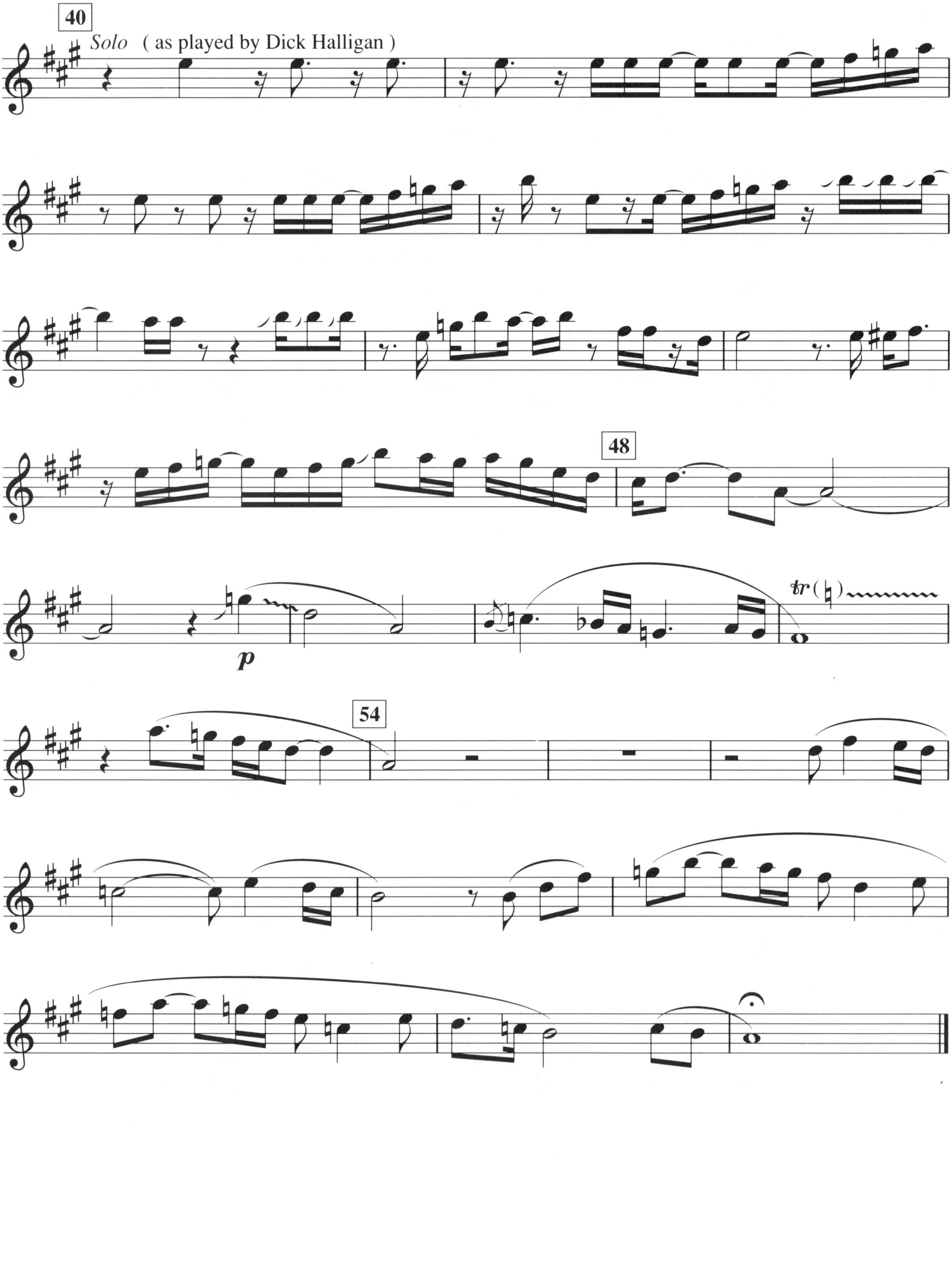
40
Solo (as played by Dick Halligan)
48
p
tr (♮)
54

SOMETIMES IN WINTER

1st B♭ TRUMPET

Words and Music by
STEVEN KATZ

SOMETIMES IN WINTER

2nd B♭ TRUMPET

Words and Music by
STEVEN KATZ

SOMETIMES IN WINTER

Words and Music by
STEVEN KATZ

TROMBONE

SPINNING WHEEL

Words and Music by
DAVID CLAYTON THOMAS

Rock ♩ = 96

Syn.
Vocal
Pno.
Bass
Drums
11
f
mf
ride a paint-ed po-ny, let the spin-ning wheel _ spin.
You got no mon-ey and you, you got no home, ______
D7+9
fill
spin-ning wheel all a - lone; _
talk-in' 'bout your trou-bles and you, you nev-er learn, _

19
Syn.
Vocal
ride a paint-ed po - ny let the spin-ning wheel _ turn. Did you find _ a di - rect - ing sign on the
Pno.
D7+9
Cadd9
Bbadd9
Bass
Fill
Drums
mp
straight and nar-row high - way? _ Would you mind _ a re - flect - ing sign? _ Just
Abadd9
Gadd9
Cadd9
Bbadd9

Syn.
Vocal
let it shine within your mind and show you the colors that are
Pno.
Abadd9
Ab/G
Bb
Bass
Fill
Drums
Syn.
cresc.
Vocal
real.
Pno.
cresc.
C
Dadd9
Bass
cresc.
Fill
Drums
cresc.

Syn.
Vocal
Pno.
Bass
Drums
f
f
f
Fill

37
Syn.
Vocal
Pno.
Bass
Drums
mf
mf
mf
slow gliss
Some - one is wait - ing
just for you,
spin - ning wheel
spin - ning true.

Syn.
Vocal
Drop all your trou-bles by the riv-er - side, catch a paint-ed po-ny on the spin-ning wheel ride.
Pno.
Bass
Drums
Fill
45
Syn.
Vocal
Pno.
Bass - ad lib. around line
(funkier)
Bass
Drums

49
Double Time
Jazz
Syn.
Vocal
Pno.
Bass
Drums
E7+9
A13
D7+9
G13
E7+9
A13
D7+9
Jazz Feel
Syn.
Vocal
Pno.
Bass
Drums
G13
E7+9
A13
D7+9
G13

65
Syn.
Vocal
Pno.
Bass
Drums
E7+9
A13
D7+9
G13
E7+9
Syn.
Vocal
Pno.
Bass
Drums
E♭7+9
D7+9
sneak in
p
Fill - set tempo

76
Rock Tempo I
Syn.
Vocal
Some-one's wait - ing just for you, spin-ning wheel spin-ning true.
Pno.
Bass
Drums
mf
Syn.
Vocal
Drop all your trou - bles by the riv - er - side, ride a paint - ed po - ny, let the spin-ning wheel fly.
Pno.
Bass
Drums

84
Syn.
Vocal
Pno.
Bass
Drums
f
Recorders (Calliope Sound)
p
Brass
Add more fills

Brass
Syn.
Vocal
Pno.
Bass
Drums
Recorders
Repeat many times and Fade
Ad lib. goofy calliope sounds
Repeat and Fade
Ad lib.

SPINNING WHEEL

B♭ TENOR SAX

Words and Music by
DAVID CLAYTON THOMAS

45
4
49
15
65
Tempo I
Rock
76
shake
84
f
2
w/recorders
p

SPINNING WHEEL

1st B♭ TRUMPET

Words and Music by
DAVID CLAYTON THOMAS

45
4
(Solo - as played by Lew Soloff)
49
F♯7+9
B13
E7+9
A13
F♯7+9
B13
E7+9
A13
F♯7+9
B13
E7+9
A13
F♯7+9
B13
E7+9
A13
65
F♯7+9
F7+9

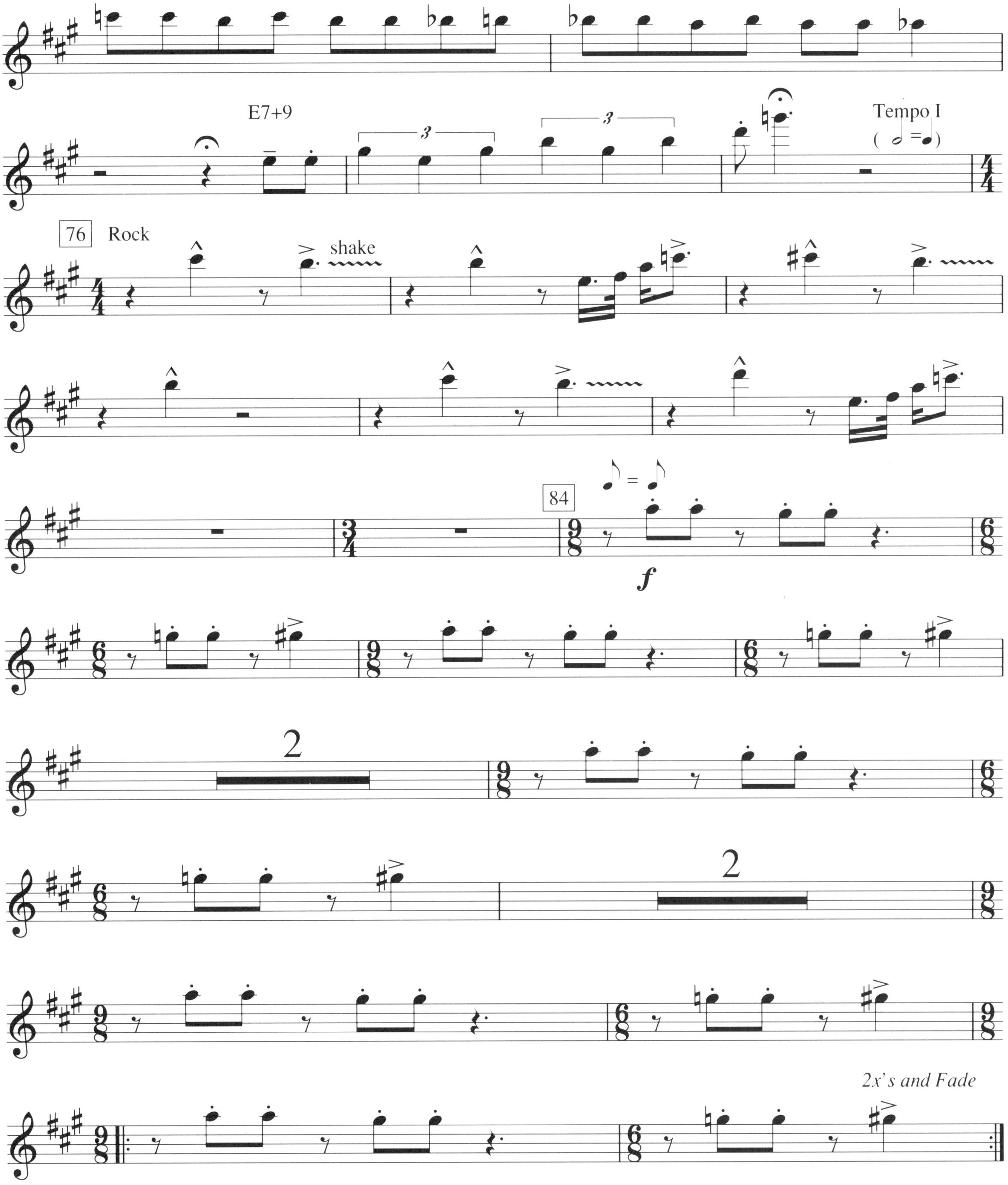
E7+9
Tempo I
76
Rock
shake
84
f
2
2
2x's and Fade

SPINNING WHEEL

2nd B♭ TRUMPET

Words and Music by
DAVID CLAYTON THOMAS

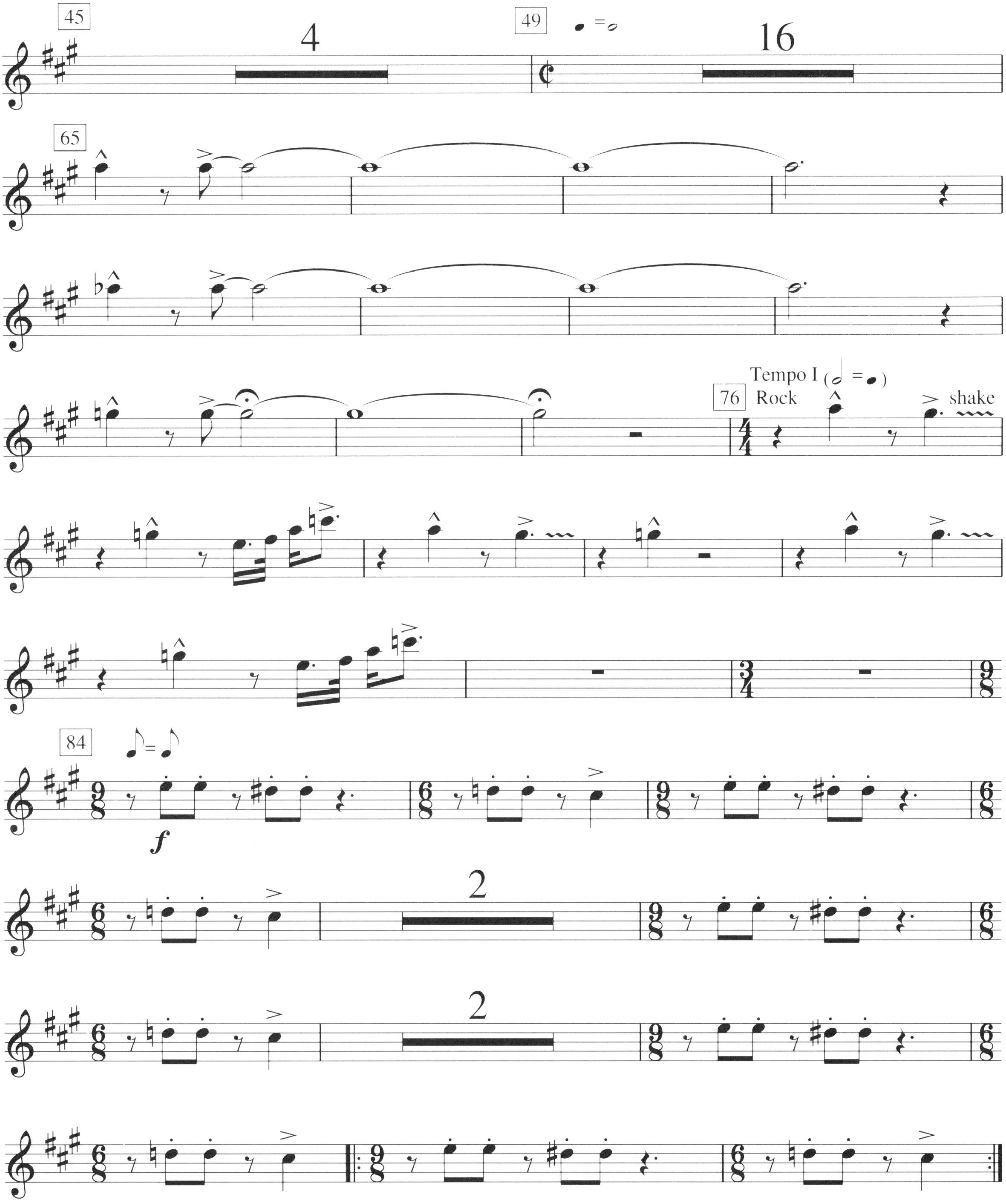
45
4
49
16
65
Tempo I
76
Rock
shake
84
2
2

SPINNING WHEEL

TROMBONE

Words and Music by
DAVID CLAYTON THOMAS

45
4
49
15
65
Tempo I
76
Rock
shake
Bass Trombone
2
2
2x's and Fade

YOU'VE MADE ME SO VERY HAPPY

Words and Music by BERRY GORDY, BRENDA HOLLOWAY,
PATRICE HOLLOWAY, and FRANK WILSON

Syn.
Vocal
just once more.
I chose you for the one,
now I'm hav - ing so much fun.
You treat - ed me so kind
Cmaj7
Dm7
Guitar
KB
Cmaj7
Dm7
Bass
Drs.
sim.
Syn.
Vocal
I'm a-bout to blow my mind.
You made me so
ver - y hap - py,
I'm so glad you
Dm7/G
Guitar
KB
Dm7/G
Bass
Fill
Drs.

21
Syn.
Vocal
came in - to my ___ life. ___
The oth - ers
Cmaj7 A7 Dm7
Guitar
KB
Cmaj7 A7 Dm7
Bass
Drs.
(4)
sim.
Syn.
Vocal
were un - true, but when it came ___ to lov - in' you ___ I'd spend my
Cmaj7 Dm7 Cmaj7 Dm7
Guitar
KB
Cmaj7 Dm7 Cmaj7 Dm7
Bass
Drs.
2
sim.

Syn.
Vocal
whole life with you. 'Cause you came and you took con - trol; _ you touched my ver - y soul. __
Cmaj7
Dm7
Guitar
KB
Cmaj7
Dm7
Bass
Drs.
Syn.
Vocal
You al - ways showed me that _ lov - ing you was where it's at. You made me ___ so
Dm7/G
Guitar
KB
Dm7/G
Bass
Drs.

Syn.
Vocal
3
ver - y hap - py, I'm so glad you came in - to my
Guitar
KB
Bass
Drs.
(4)

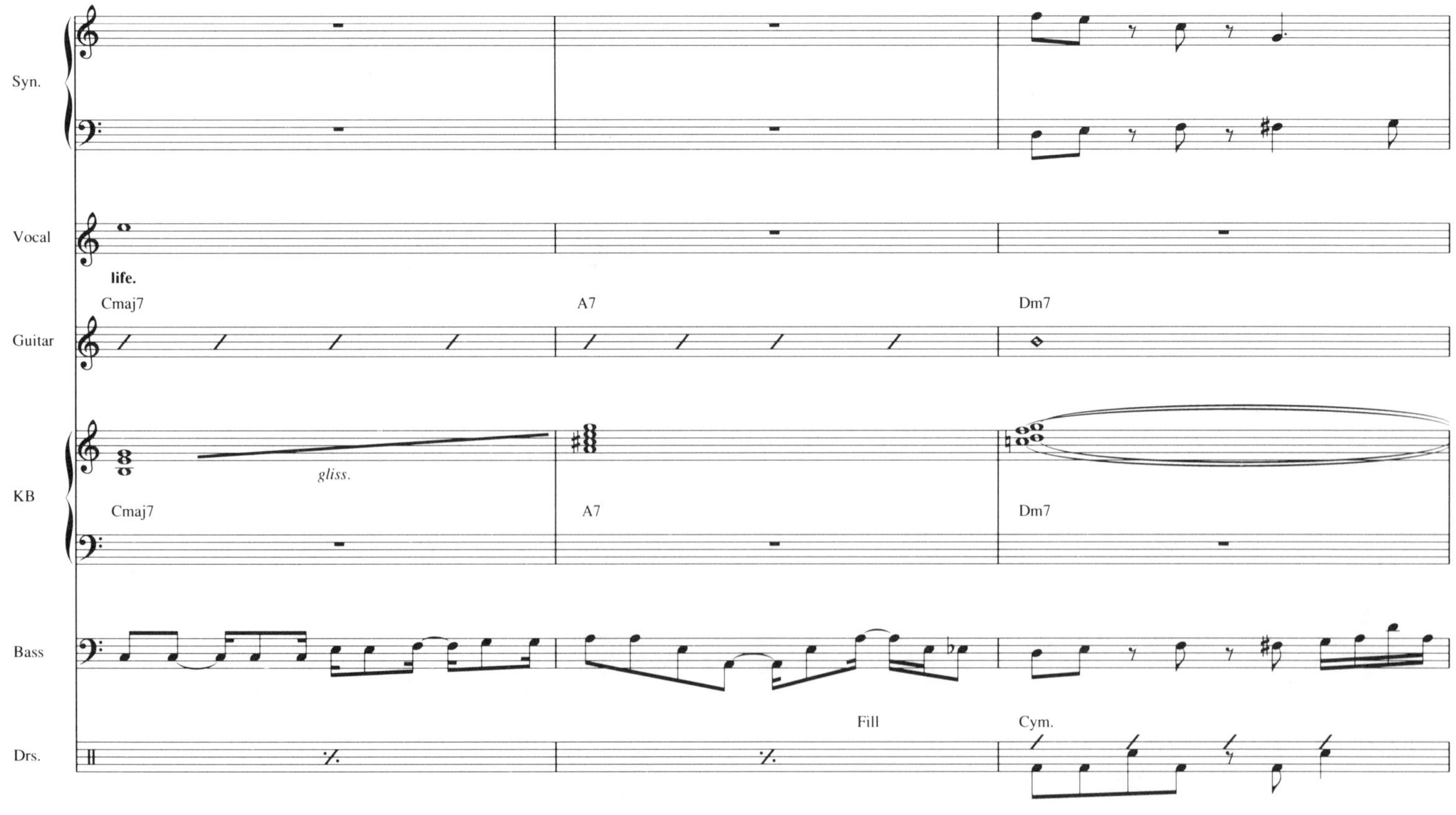
Syn.
Vocal
life.
Cmaj7 A7 Dm7
Guitar
KB
gliss.
Cmaj7 A7 Dm7
Bass
Fill
Cym.
Drs.

Syn.
Vocal
Thank you ba - by!
Yeah,
Guitar
KB
Bass
Drs.
(4)
43
yeah.
I love you so much it seems,
Cmaj7
A7
long fall
B♭
Hat
p

Syn.
Vocal
you're e-ven in my dreams, I can hear you, yeah I can hear you call-ing me.
Guitar
KB
F
C
Bass
Drs.
(4)
I'm so in love with you; all I ev-er want to do is thank you ba-by,
Bb
Dm7
Fill

51
Syn.
Vocal
thank you ba - by.
Guitar
KB
Dm7/G
Dm(add9)
Em(add9)
Bass
Drs.
Syn.
Vocal
Guitar
KB
Fmaj7
G♭dim
Gm
Am
B♭
Bass
Drs.

61
Syn.
Vocal
Guitar
KB
Bass
Drs.
Dm
Cm
Dm
E♭m
Csus
Dm
Cm
Dm
E♭m
Fill
Fill
D♭m
E♭m
Dm
E♭m
D♭
D♭m
E♭m
Dm
E♭m
D♭
(4)

69
Syn.
Vocal
You made me so ver - y hap - py,
E♭m7
Guitar
KB
E♭m7
Bass
Drs.
Syn.
Vocal
I'm so glad you came in - to my life.
D♭maj7
B♭7
Guitar
KB
D♭maj7
B♭7
Bass
Drs.
Fill
Fill

Syn.
Vocal
You made me so, ver - y hap - py, you made me so,
E♭m7 G♭m6 Fm7
Guitar
KB
E♭m7 G♭m6 Fm7
Bass
Drs.
Fill
Syn.
Vocal
so ver - y hap - py ba - by, I'm so glad you came in - to my
B♭7♭5 E♭m7 A♭7♭5
Guitar
KB
gliss.
B♭7♭5 E♭m7 A♭7♭5 N.C.
Bass
Drs.
(4)

82
Syn.
Vocal
life.
Mmm,
thank you, girl.
Guitar
organ
G♭ (add9)
C♭maj7(6)
KB
piano
Bass
Drs.
Repeat and Fade
tacet 1st & 2nd x
tacet 1st & 2nd x
* ad lib spoken words
8 va
C♭maj7(6)
ad lib on fade
cym.
tacet 1st & 2nd x

YOU'VE MADE ME SO VERY HAPPY

E♭ ALTO SAX

Words and Music by BERRY GORDY, BRENDA HOLLOWAY,
PATRICE HOLLOWAY, and FRANK WILSON

51
5
61
69
82
4
tacet 1st & 2nd x
Repeat and Fade

YOU'VE MADE ME SO VERY HAPPY

B♭ TRUMPET 1

Words and Music by BERRY GORDY, BRENDA HOLLOWAY,
PATRICE HOLLOWAY, and FRANK WILSON

51
5
61
69
82
4
To Harmon
tacet 1st & 2nd x
Repeat and Fade

YOU'VE MADE ME SO VERY HAPPY

B♭ TRUMPET 2

Words and Music by BERRY GORDY, BRENDA HOLLOWAY,
PATRICE HOLLOWAY, and FRANK WILSON

51
5
61
69
82
4
tacet 1st & 2nd x
Repeat and Fade

YOU'VE MADE ME SO VERY HAPPY

TROMBONE

Words and Music by BERRY GORDY, BRENDA HOLLOWAY,
PATRICE HOLLOWAY, and FRANK WILSON

51
5
61
69
82
4
tacet 1st & 2nd x
Repeat and Fade

ARTIST TRANSCRIPTIONS™

Artist Transcriptions are authentic, note-for-note transcriptions of the music of the hottest wind, guitar and keyboard artists. These outstanding, accurate arrangements are in an easy-to-read format which includes all essential lines. Artist Transcriptions can be used to perform or reference.

Chick Corea — Light Years
Transcriptions to the songs on the "Light Years" album. This book uses Chick's special chord notation for various C instruments. It features 12 songs, including: Hymn Of The Heart • Light Years • Prism • Second Sight • and more.
00674305 .... $14.95

Chick Corea — Eye Of The Beholder
Includes all of the songs on the album, "Eye Of The Beholder," transcribed directly from Chick's score. Included is Chick's special chord notation for piano, synthesizer, sax, guitar, bass and drums.
00660007 .... $14.95

The David Sanborn Collection
This is a collection of 15 transcriptions of this great sax player's best. Songs include: A Change Of Heart • Hideaway • Straight To The Heart • and more.
00675000 .... $12.95

Wes Montgomery Transcriptions
A definitive collection of full transcriptions by one of the most classic jazz innovators the guitar world has ever seen. Special section gives an insight into Wes' playing concepts and techniques. 15 songs, including: Boss City • Four On Six • Movin' Wes Part I & Part II • Serene • The Thumb • Twisted Blues.
00675536 .... $14.95

Transcribed SCORES™

Transcribed scores are vocal and instrumental arrangements of music from some of the greatest groups in music. These excellent publications feature transcribed parts for lead vocals, backup vocals — and all of the various instruments used in each specific recording session. All songs are arranged exactly the way the artists recorded them.

The Best Of Blood Sweat & Tears
Seven hits from the quintessential jazz/rock group. Every note and nuance...vocal lines, brass, sax, keyboard, bass and drums, plus a synthesizer line for the auxiliary instruments (each sound clearly identified). And When I Die • God Bless' The Child • Go Down Gamblin' • Lucretia MacEvil • Sometimes In Winter • Spinning Wheel • You've Made Me So Very Happy.
00673208 .... $16.95

The Beatles — The Blue Book
Can't Buy Me Love • Day Tripper • Here Comes The Sun • Hey Jude • Lady Madonna • Penny Lane • Yesterday.
00674280 .... $9.95

The Beatles — The Red Book
All You Need Is Love • Back In The U.S.S.R. • Good Day Sunshine • The Long And Winding Road • Michelle • Paperback Writer • Please Please Me.
00675422 .... $9.95

The Beatles — The Yellow Book
A Day In The Life • Eight Days A Week • Eleanor Rigby • A Hard Day's Night • Hello, Goodbye • I Feel Fine • Something.
00673145 .... $9.95

The Beatles — The Green Book
Come Together • Got To Get You Into My Life • I Saw Her Standing Ther
• In My Life • Let It Be • Strawberry Fields Forever • Ticket To Ride.
00673395 .... $9.

The Best Of Spyro Gyra
A chronology of favorite tunes from this award-winning jazz group.
Note-for-note scores for sax, keyboards, mallets, guitar, bass, percu
drums. 10 tunes, including: Shaker Song • Morning Dance • C
The Sun • Joy Ride.
00675170 ....

Sting — Nothing Like The Sun
Matching folio to the popular LP by Sting, this collection c
plete instrument-for-instrument transcriptions for all 12 sc
on the album. Songs include: Be Still My Beating Heart •
In New York • Straight To My Heart • and more.
00674655 ....

Best Of Weather Report
A collection of 14 of their very best, including: Mysterious Tr
Birdland • Palladium • Mr. Gone • Badia/Boogie Woogie W
Medley • Brown Street • 8:30.
00675520 .... $

Yellow Jackets — Four Corners
Complete instrument-for-instrument transcriptions for this Gramm
Award winning jazz/fusion group. Instrumentation includes
keyboards, saxophone, bass and drums. Features all 10 tunes fron
the LP, including the hit "Mile High" and the bonus tune from the
CD/cassette, "Indigo."
00675800 .... $16.9

For more information,
see your local music dealer, or write to:

HL Hal Leonard Publishing Corporation
P.O. Box 13819 Milwaukee, Wisconsin 53213